A LINE IN THE SNOW
The Battle for ANWR
(The Arctic National Wildlife Refuge)

A LINE IN THE SNOW
The Battle for ANWR
(The Arctic National Wildlife Refuge)

Michael Farrar

iUniverse, Inc.
New York   Bloomington

A Line in the Snow
The Battle for the Arctic National Wildlife Refuge (ANWR)

iUniverse books may be ordered through booksellers or by contacting:

iUniverse
1663 Liberty Drive
Bloomington, IN 47403
www.iuniverse.com
1-800-Authors (1-800-288-4677)

Because of the dynamic nature of the Internet, any Web addresses or links contained in this book may have changed since publication and may no longer be valid. The views expressed in this work are solely those of the author and do not necessarily reflect the views of the publisher, and the publisher hereby disclaims any responsibility for them.

ISBN: 978-1-4401-6140-7 (sc)
ISBN: 978-1-4401-6138-4 (dj)
ISBN: 978-1-4401-6139-1 (ebook)

Printed in the United States of America

iUniverse rev. date: 9/23/2009

To Claudia, Shane, and Dakota

A LINE IN THE SNOW
The Battle for ANWR
(The Arctic National Wildlife Refuge)

CONTENTS

Introduction xi

I   Prudhoe Bay: Lessons Learned 1

II   Alaska: The Path to Statehood 9

III The Creation of ANWR 13

IV   The 1002 Area Hydrocarbon Resource Potential 17

V   ANWR Comprehensive Conservation Plan and
     Environmental Impact Statement 25

VI   Environmental Considerations 33
     Ecology 33
     Climate 35
     Air and Water Quality 36
     Geology of the North Slope 36
     Vegetation 39
     Fish and Wildlife 39
     Birds 40
     Marine Mammals 41
     Terrestrial Mammals 44

VII The Porcupine Caribou Herd 49

STAKEHOLDERS 55

VIII The Federal Government 57
     Executive Branch 57
     Department of the Interior U.S. Fish and Wildlife Service
     (USFWS) 59
     Department of the Interior U.S. Geological Survey (USGS) . 61
     U.S. Department of Energy (DOE) 62

Environmental Protection Agency (EPA). 67
Legislative Branch: History of Legislative Activity 67
Congressional Activists. 74

IX   State of Alaska 79
The Permanent Fund and Revenue Distribution 79
Alaskan Sentiment 80
Alaskan Job Growth 82
Native Alaskans The Arctic Slope Regional Corporation . . . 83
Kaktovik 84
The Gwich'in. 88

X   Canada. 93

XI   Wildlife, Environmental, and Conservation Organizations. . 97
Alaska Coalition 98
Alaska Wilderness League 100
Center for Biological Diversity. 100
Environmental Defense Fund 101
Green Century Capital Management. 102
Greenpeace. 103
The Nature Conservancy. 103
Natural Resources Defense Council 105
The Sierra Club 106
U.S. PIRG 107
World Wildlife Fund. 107

XII Pro-Development Constituents 109
Energy Companies. 109
BP 110
ConocoPhillips. 111
Chevron 112
Anadarko 114
ExxonMobil 115
The American Petroleum Institute 116
Arctic Power 118
Think Tanks: The Heritage Foundation and the National
Defense Council Foundation. 119

XIII The American Public: Perceptions and Polls 121

XIV Rhetoric versus Reality 127

XV Possible Solutions 143

XVI Conclusion 149

References 153

Index 164

COVER IMAGES
Front: Trans Alaska Pipeline System (TAPS)
Back: A Line Of Caribou In The Snow

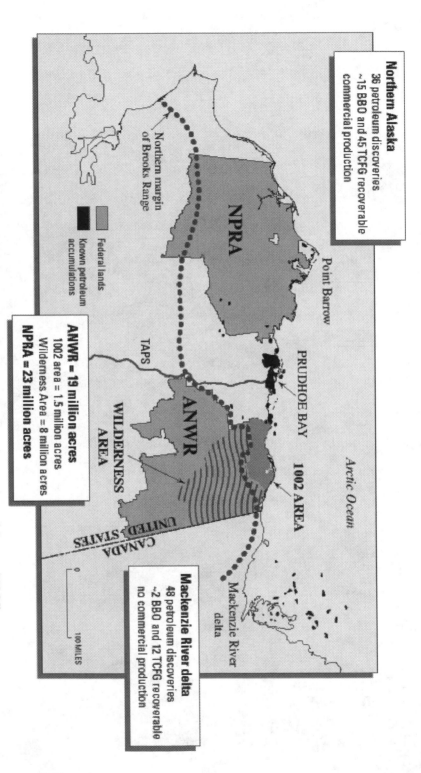

Northern Alaska
36 petroleum discoveries
~15 BBO and 45 TCFG recoverable
commercial production

Point Barrow

NPRA

Northern margin
of Brooks Range

Federal lands

Known petroleum
accumulations

Arctic Ocean

PRUDHOE BAY

1002 AREA

TAPS

ANWR

WILDERNESS
AREA

ANWR = 19 million acres
1002 area = 1.5 million acres
Wilderness Area = 8 million acres
NPRA = 23 million acres

UNITED STATES
CANADA

Mackenzie River
delta

Mackenzie River delta
48 petroleum discoveries
~2 BBO and 12 TCFG recoverable
no commercial production

0   100 MILES

North Slope Oil Discoveries and ANWR Source: U.S. Geological Survey (USGS)

A LINE IN THE SNOW:
The Battle For ANWR

Introduction

THE ARCTIC NATIONAL WILDLIFE Refuge (ANWR) consists of more than 19 million acres of federal territory situated in northeast Alaska, bordering Canada's Yukon Territory. While the vast majority of the Refuge is already protected from development, 1.5 million acres are potentially available for exploration, subject to congressional authorization. Energy companies have maintained that vast oil reserves, as much as 10 billion barrels, may lie within ANWR. These companies have petitioned the federal government for access. Environmental organizations proclaim that the coastal plain of ANWR represents a unique and delicate ecosystem that would be irreparably damaged if hydrocarbon exploration and production were allowed. They want the land in question to be declared a Wilderness Area, which would effectively prohibit development.

The debate has raged in Congress since the 1980s, with no end in sight.

Bills were frequently introduced in the Republican-dominated Congress prior to 2007 to open ANWR to exploration licensing, but to no avail. Oil prices peaked at the $145 per barrel mark for the first time in the summer of 2008, and gas prices hovered around $4.00 per gallon. Yet, despite the public outcry for relief and the efforts of the Bush administration and the Republicans in Congress to produce an energy policy that reduced U.S. dependence on foreign oil, no bills have succeeded in passing. How was this possible? What is it about ANWR that seems to have galvanized public opinion to declare it off limits for petroleum exploration? Have environmental organizations succeeded in portraying ANWR as the last great American frontier and achieved the political support required to defeat what appeared to many energy advocates as a sure thing?

Has ANWR become the definitive "line in the snow" between opponents and advocates of further energy exploration in the United States?

This book attempts to address this very question in a thorough and objective manner. It is nonpartisan in its approach. Rather, the purpose is to undertake a comprehensive examination of ANWR, the stakeholders, their claims and possible biases, and to present this information to the readers so that they may have an informed basis for determining the outcome of this monumental debate.

At the same time, however, one cannot help but express dismay and even outrage at the inability of the Congress, past and present, to act on this critical issue. ANWR has been debated in Congress for more than two decades without resolution. Countless hearings have been held, a plethora of bills introduced, vast sums of money and time wasted on study after study; all to no avail. One begins to suspect that our country's leaders do not truly seek a solution, preferring instead to continuously employ ANWR as a political litmus test for determining environmental versus energy policies. It is as if ANWR has become the proverbial "third rail" of environmental politics.

The debate over whether to open the coastal plain of ANWR for development has enveloped far more than energy companies and conservation groups. Although it is federal territory, Alaska and its citizens would benefit greatly from development, both in terms of jobs and revenues. As the oil fields at Prudhoe Bay steadily decline, threatening to permanently shut down the Trans Alaskan Pipeline, additional production from ANWR of as much as 1 million barrels of oil per day (MMBOPD) would breathe new life into Alaska's North Slope and provide a major boost to the Alaskan economy. Conservative think tanks whose agenda is to promote energy security, have joined forces with the pro-development groups, lobbying hard in Washington for favorable action.

However, environmental organizations have also found unlikely allies in some native Alaskan communities and among national sporting associations. The Gwich'in of Alaska and Canada have expressed concerns about the impact of development on their way of life, especially as it might impact the viability of the Porcupine caribou herd as the herd migrates and calves along the Arctic coastal plain. The sporting associations view ANWR as a paradise for hunting and fishing, and feel that any development would impinge on the wilderness aspect of the entire Refuge. Although individual motives may be disparate, the ultimate objective is the same: a ban on drilling.

Senators and congressional representatives from states on the Pacific and Atlantic coasts are particularly sensitive to discussions regarding ANWR. They have come to view ANWR as the front line in the war against further offshore development. So much effort has been expended in portraying ANWR as America's last great frontier that it would be difficult to oppose exploration leasing in federal waters off California, Florida, and elsewhere along the U.S. outer continental shelves if ANWR was legislated for development. As ANWR goes, so goes the rest. Hence, even when the question of more drilling arises in Congress, ANWR is usually the very first item stricken from the discussion.

What would it take for Congress to act decisively on this matter? Only one thing seems to galvanize Congress: a crisis. Not just any crisis, but one that cuts across party lines, a crisis so large that it cannot be simply studied and debated, or ignored until it goes away: a crisis that will throw them out of office come the next election cycle if something is not done now. And that crisis is now upon us: the rapid, skyrocketing cost of energy. All the eloquent speeches and fiery debate over the past twenty years about energy security and achieving independence from foreign oil meant little until Americans directly felt the economic impact at the pump and in their utility bills. It is truly unfortunate that an issue must take on crisis proportions before it is genuinely addressed by our nation's leaders. When this occurs, one side of the debate generally is given far more weight than if it were deliberated under calmer conditions. Since this crisis is about energy and the economy, environmental concerns may be downplayed. Had the crisis been another oil spill along the lines of the *Exxon Valdez*, energy security concerns would most likely be overlooked.

While there may be an energy shortage, there is certainly no shortage of rhetoric coming from all sides. The distortions and misrepresentations have made it nearly impossible for the interested observer to distinguish fact from fiction. An entire chapter is devoted to addressing the rhetoric and exaggerated claims that emanate from the stakeholders. Yet the biggest stakeholder remains largely silent. It is the American public. They are the true property owners. ANWR may reside in Alaska, but it is federal, not state, territory. ANWR is not the excusive domain of the energy companies or the environmental groups with their respective alliances. ANWR belongs to us. It is ours to decide the outcome.

This author maintains a deep and passionate interest in ANWR. As both an exploration geologist and an environmentalist, I feel it is critically important that we address the complex issues that surround the Refuge in a straightforward, comprehensive manner. The reason I undertook this challenge was simply so that one could locate a single source that was both thorough and unbiased. There are publications by the Congressional Research Service (CRS) on the legislative aspects of ANWR, as well as reports by the U.S. Geological Survey (USGS) and the U.S. Fish and Wildlife Service (USFWS). Each of these documents focuses on a single aspect of the great debate. There are also articles by various interest groups, but objectivity is often lacking. There simply does not exist a thoroughly comprehensive and objective treatise on the complex issues regarding ANWR, until now.

I have been to Alaska on numerous occasions, including several visits to the Prudhoe Bay complex of oil fields immediately adjacent to ANWR. I have witnessed firsthand what can and cannot be done on Alaska's Arctic coastal plain. I have also seen the majestic beauty that spans Alaska, from the coastal plain on the North Slope to the mountain ranges and glaciers, fiords and forests, all teeming with wildlife. It truly represents an inspiring panoply of environmental diversity. Preserving that diversity is important. So is energy security.

This matter is far too important to allow another twenty years to slip by without resolution. It is far too significant to let Congress waste more precious time and money by conducting endless hearings and by allowing legislation to languish in committees. It is far too critical to let this great resource be held in suspension indefinitely without knowing the full extent of all the issues that encompass this great debate.

This book will appeal to conservation organizations and energy advocates, political analysts, academicians, the media (as it relates to energy policy), and the general public who desperately hunger for more than a thirty-second sound bite on an issue that profoundly impacts their daily lives.

Chapter I: Prudhoe Bay: Lessons Learned

Prudhoe Bay Field: Courtesy of U.S. Fish and Wildlife Service (USFWS)

IT WAS EARLY SPRING of 1990, but Prudhoe Bay was still locked in an icy embrace. As exploration advisor for ARCO International, I was escorting a group of six Russian engineers and geoscientists to the North Slope. These men hailed from Archangelsk in northern Russia. At latitude sixty-four degrees north, they were slightly below the Arctic Circle but experienced similar operating conditions to Alaska's North Slope and Prudhoe Bay. The distinguished delegation, all men, represented senior-level geologists, geophysicists, and drilling and reservoir engineers from the Russian state-owned company Archangelsk Geologia. They were well educated, experienced, and hardened by the extreme conditions in which they had to operate in their mission to recover oil and gas reserves from the Timan Pechora Basin. They knew the West had better

1

technology and resources, and seizing the advantage from President Gorbachev's open policies of *glasnost* and *perestroika*, they were anxious to bring those resources back home.

Our flight to Anchorage, the jumping-off point for Prudhoe Bay, arrived late at night. It was already past midnight by the time we were all checked into the Captain Cook Hotel in downtown Anchorage. Knowing that we had a very early start the next morning, I was ready to collapse in my bed and get a few miserly hours of rest. It was not meant to be. A knock on my door from Sergei, the youngest of the group and with the greatest command of the English language, brought an invitation to join the Russians in a little celebration upon arriving in the United States. None had ever been to the United States before, so for them it was a cause for celebration. Being the host, I could not refuse. I followed Sergei to Anatoly's room, where a sumptuous feast of dried meats, bricks of caviar, vodka, and Russian brandy was spread out before me. These men were ready to party. I could only marvel at their stamina as we consumed nearly everything in sight, including the vodka (I cannot recall what happened to the brandy). It was a bonding moment that set the course for the days ahead. At that very moment, we were all comrades. I stumbled back to my room, where the alarm went off about thirty minutes later.

I showered and dressed and joined my comrades at the hotel restaurant for a hearty breakfast. They were already there, jovial and scarfing down a lumberjack feast of several thousand calories. The events of a few short hours ago had done little to dull their appetite. I was still hung over but the coffee brought me back to life.

At the airport in Anchorage, we joined the queue of oil field workers headed for the North Slope via a charter flight. The men and women who work on the North Slope, whether it be Prudhoe Bay or the other fields, usually work on a rotating basis of either seven or fourteen days: seven days on and seven days off. It is bachelor-status only on the North Slope. While this arrangement can seem hard on families, most have adjusted, and many seem to enjoy it, utilizing their time off to spend more time together, take vacations or work on projects.

Security is tight. No firearms or alcohol are allowed at Prudhoe Bay, and there is a special police force to enforce the rules. Given the dangerous nature of the work on the North Slope, and the volumes of oil and natural gas that are processed on a daily basis, guns and liquor would be a recipe for disaster. So, there we were at the check-in desk for the flight, and one of the Russians mentioned that he still had a few bottles of vodka in his luggage. To them, it was as natural to have a bottle of vodka as it is for us to carry a bottle of water. Keep in mind that this was a decade before the September 11, 2001, attack that forever changed the way we fly. I dutifully notified the airline personnel of the situation, explaining that these were guests in our country and unaware of the rules. The attendant quickly grasped the diplomatic delicacy of the situation and offered to hold the vodka at the airport until we returned from Prudhoe (made me suspect she had witnessed these situations before).

Once on the plane, we settled back for the two-hour flight to the airstrip at Prudhoe Bay. Relishing the idea of a quick nap, I had just dozed off when Sergei nudged my arm. It turned out that one member of the delegation had just remembered that he had some more vodka and brandy in his carry-on luggage.

"Good God!" I thought. "Just how much booze do these guys carry? Do they have any room at all for clothes, like underwear?"

Having been to Prudhoe Bay before, I knew our luggage would be inspected by the security detail immediately upon our arrival. And if they found contraband of any sort, whether it be alcohol, firearms, or drugs, we would be detained at the terminal and put on the next flight back. In addition, criminal prosecution was not out of the realm of possibilities. I envisioned my career with ARCO coming to an abrupt and undignified end. I would surely be fired for this serious security breach.

Rather than wait until we landed, I figured it best to notify the flight crew. I explained the situation: Russian delegation, guests in our country, hosted by ARCO, didn't know the rules, etc. The flight crew were a little shocked but took it all in stride. They immediately notified security at Prudhoe Bay, who were waiting in force upon our departure from the plane. We were all ushered into a special examination room, where the security detail went through every single bag and confiscated the half-dozen or so bottles of Russian vodka and brandy. Then, before our eyes, they opened every bottle and poured the contents down the sink. They then wished us a pleasant visit and sent us on our way. By then, a stiff drink would have received an enthusiastic reception.

Over the ensuing forty-eight hours, the Russians witnessed just about every ongoing operation on the North Slope. They ate and slept at the accommodation module at Kuparuk Field, the home-away-from-home for many of the workers, both male and female. The food was well prepared, readily available, and abundant. The facility included recreation rooms, a movie theater, and exercise rooms.

In fact, all of the facilities were spotless and well maintained. It was apparent that the workers on the North Slope took their jobs seriously and with a degree of pride. The Russians toured an exploration drill rig, production facilities, and processing plants. They saw the discovery well and the Trans Alaskan Pipeline System (TAPS), including Pump Station #1, where the oil commences its 800-mile journey to the terminals at Valdez. Presentations were made regarding day-to-day operations, safety procedures, waste disposal, and working conditions. Having observed the difficult and dangerous conditions under which the Russians had to operate in Archangelsk, I was keenly aware of the stark contrast that was laid out before them. Between presentations, the men would often huddle and a very animated conversation would break out. With what little Russian I understood, and it was indeed very little, I knew they were comparing their lives to those of the workers on the North Slope. Initially, I thought they might be wondering how different their lives would have been had they been born in America. However, it soon became apparent that they were really imagining how different their lives would be if they could create the same living and working conditions back home. After all, they were Russians and proud of it. They simply wanted a better life for themselves, their families, and their community.

A few days later, we departed Prudhoe Bay for the long trek back to Plano, Texas, which was headquarters for ARCO International. After a brief meeting with ARCO's president, another facility tour, and a round of picture taking, we sat down to business. The Russians wasted no time. Anatoly, the senior member of the delegation and a drilling engineer, spoke first. Like most drillers worldwide, Anatoly was brief, almost to the point of being blunt (must be an unwritten job requirement for drillers). He spoke in Russian; Sergei translated.

Anatoly wanted ARCO to partner with his company, Archangelsk Geologia, to explore and develop the entire Timan Pechora Basin. He was offering us an exclusive on an entire geologic basin that was already a known hydrocarbon-producing province. I nearly fell off my chair. This was practically unheard of in the rest of the world, where most basins are carved up into small blocks and bid out for large sums of money, depending on their level of prospectivity.

The potential was enormous. So were the risks. Not so much from a technical perspective, as we had already evaluated the Timan Pechora Basin and knew we could bring technology to bear on tapping substantial oil and gas reserves in an environmentally better way than was currently being employed. And we knew that the benefits would accrue, not just to ARCO, but to the residents of Archangelsk. However, the political risks were significant. Russia had yet to adopt laws regarding foreign investment in the oil and gas sector. There was a great deal of uncertainty regarding not only the kind of contracts that should apply, but whether the Russian government would recognize these contracts and give them the necessary backing of the rule of law that would be universally recognized.

ARCO executives felt the political risks were too high to gamble the company's assets and declined the seemingly generous offer. Both the Russians and those of us who had worked on the project were devastated. At the time, I felt we had passed on a company-making opportunity. In retrospect, it turned out to be a good decision. The Russian government under Vladimir Putin subsequently clawed back many of the contracts that had been executed, squeezing out the American and European partners to many joint ventures after substantial investments had been made.

Despite our little misadventure with the Russians, I never forgot how impressed they were with operations on the North Slope. And it wasn't just the technology that was a factor, it was very much the safety and environmental standards that were employed. It was also the working conditions and treatment of the employees. It was how they felt life should also be for them, and it was a valuable lesson for me in how far we have advanced since the first discovery well was drilled in 1968 and field development took place during the 1970s.

In those early years, our understanding of operating under arctic conditions was minimal. Seismic lines cut through the tundra, some of which are still visible today. Haul roads were bulldozed, exposing the permafrost to seasonal melting and creating a quagmire in the tundra. Drill pads for a single well were as large as forty-four acres, resulting in a sprawling field complex. Knowledge regarding the impact of field development on local wildlife was scant, thus requiring lengthy, costly, and necessary environmental impact statements (EISs). The footprint of the early fields was large and extended across a broad swath of the North Slope. The impact on wildlife appears to have been minimal, but eternal vigilance is warranted when interacting with the delicate arctic ecosystems.

Fortunately, the lessons learned from the mistakes of the early days on the North Slope have resulted in numerous improvements, both from both an operating and an environmental perspective.

Drill pads are now on the order of five to seven acres, casting a much smaller footprint. More significantly, however, is the ability to drill multiple wells from a single drill pad. As many as thirty-plus wells could be directionally drilled from a single pad. Hence, the field footprint is also substantially reduced. In addition, the drilling fluids and well cuttings are now contained and reinjected, whereas early on, they were placed in nearby surface pits.

Exploration activities, including seismic programs and exploratory wells, are limited to the winter months when ice pads can be constructed for the wells and the seismic impact over the frozen tundra is substantially reduced.

Seasonal limitations are also placed on exploration and construction activities in order to protect local wildlife, particularly during sensitive breeding and migration periods.

Low-impact cat trains for transporting workers and equipment are now employed, as opposed to standard vehicles which leave imprints.

Seismic cat train: Courtesy of USFWS

Temporary ice roads and airstrips are also constructed when needed, especially during the exploration or early construction phase of a project.

Permanent roads and pipelines are now designed with an eye toward minimal impact on local and migratory wildlife, fish, and fresh water sources.

All waste products generated on the North Slope are now treated, contained, and disposed of in accordance with strict regulations.

Spill monitoring and reporting, as well as air and water quality monitoring, are now standard procedures on the North Slope and have been for some time.

Alpine Field is a good example of improvements made over the years. The field, which commenced production in 2000, is located approximately forty miles west of Kuparuk Field. Benefiting from directional drilling, zero waste discharge, and roadless development, the 40,000-acre field has an environmental footprint of only 97 acres.

Certainly, numerous improvements over the last four decades have been made on the North Slope. Did the energy companies come by these enhancements on their own volition, or were they dragged, kicking and screaming, by environmental organizations and regulatory agencies? It's probably a little bit of both. What is important, however, is that it happened. It bodes well for any future development that might take place on the North Slope, whether it be in ANWR or elsewhere.

Chapter II: Alaska: The Path to Statehood

ALASKA IS NO STRANGER to political controversy. Most texts in American history contain a terse narrative on the 1867 purchase of Alaska from Russia for $7.2 million. The purchase was orchestrated by U.S. Secretary of State William Seward. As most Americans at that time perceived little or no value in the Alaskan Territory, the purchase was widely referred to as "Seward's Folly."

Seward was ridiculed for this purchase, but scant attention has been devoted as to why the purchase was made in the first place. It followed precipitously on the heels of the British North America Act of 1867. This act created one dominion under the name of "Canada" which was subject to the British Crown. Fearing unchecked British colonialism in the north, Seward moved to halt further British expansion by negotiating the purchase of 586,000 square miles from Imperial Russia. This purchase is celebrated by Alaskans on the last Monday in March, called "Seward's Day."

Alaska was initially designated a Customs District of the United States. The American flag was first raised over Alaska on October 18, 1867, which is now commemorated as "Alaska Day." As a Customs District, the U.S. Navy governed it and was responsible for maintaining civil order. In 1884, the First Organic Act was passed. This law conferred a civil and judicial status upon the district. A legal code was established and administered by judges and marshals. It became an official U.S. territory in 1912 with congressional passage of the Second Organic Act.

Scant attention was given Alaska until gold was discovered, setting off the Klondike gold rush of the 1890s. With the rapid infusion of settlers also came the discovery of other vast resources, such as minerals, fish, and fur. Syndicates, which included the likes of J. P. Morgan and

Guggenheim, sprang up in the early 1900s and controlled shipping and rail transportation in and out of Alaska. In addition, they also controlled the burgeoning salmon canning industry.

These syndicates, through their powerful Washington influences, managed to stave off Alaskan self-rule efforts for the better part of a decade.

However, in 1910, a little-known event, the Ballinger-Pinchot affair, made public the illegal award of multiple Alaskan coal land claims. The congressional investigation that ensued resulted in the demise of the powerful syndicates and once again elevated Alaska into the national political spotlight. It also paved the way for obtaining territorial status in 1912, which, among other provisions, allowed the formation of a state legislature. Nonetheless, Congress maintained a final say on all relevant legislative action, and the federal government retained regulatory authority over the Alaskan fish and game industries. Alaska was represented in Congress by a single territorial delegate.

At the beginning of the twentieth century, oil seeps along the Arctic coastal plain in northern Alaska were discovered. This led to the federal government declaring a 23-million-acre Naval Petroleum Reserve in the northwestern part of the Arctic coastal plain in 1923. This area was subsequently renamed the National Petroleum Reserve -Alaska (NPR-A), and was intended to secure a stable supply of oil in the future. Oil fields have subsequently been discovered and developed in NPR-A.

The territory briefly dropped off the national radar screen in the late 1920s and 1930s. This period was interspersed by a combination of jurisdictional disputes between the administrative regions, bickering amongst native Alaskans, and finally, the Great Depression. Some efforts were made to colonize (populate) Alaska through related New Deal programs in the 1930s, but these were largely unsuccessful.

Alaska was once again thrust onto the national stage with the advent of World War II. Anticipating a Japanese military buildup in the Pacific, in 1940 Congress authorized funds for military installations and highways in Alaska. The U.S. government also declared the 48.8-million-acre North Slope under federal jurisdiction for military reasons. Japan invaded Alaska in June 1942 and occupied two islands in the Aleutian Island chain: Attu and Kiska. The Japanese also conducted an aerial attack on the military base at Dutch Harbor on Amaknak Island, inflicting approximately one hundred casualties. By the time the U.S. military mounted a counterattack, the Japanese had evacuated the islands. Since then, the military has played a major role in Alaska's economy. By 1943, U.S. military personnel in Alaska outnumbered the local population. Even after World War II, cold war concerns resulted in a heavy military presence in the Territory, as Alaska was at the forefront of the Distant Early Warning (DEW) Line.

Following World War II, the territorial governor, the congressional delegate, and numerous business entities conducted a major drive to obtain statehood status. It was felt that statehood would bring badly needed infrastructure improvements, as well as a resolution of aboriginal status and land ownership rights. The Alaska Statehood Association was formed in 1946 to essentially lobby Congress for statehood. The association was composed primarily of Alaskan citizens and businesses. This organization later merged with the Alaska Statehood Committee in 1949, which was a much larger entity and included prominent figures outside of Alaska. The committee managed to propel Alaska's plight once again into the national spotlight, and in 1950 a statehood bill was introduced in Congress. The bill passed in the House but was defeated in the Senate. Interestingly, it was defeated by a coalition of conservative Republicans and Democrats over fears that the new state would tend to vote for liberal Democratic positions.

The Korean conflict erupted in 1950 and effectively sidelined efforts for statehood status until the cessation of hostilities in 1952. By now, there was a growing populist movement for statehood from both within Alaska and the lower forty-eight states. Despite the popular movement, in 1954 President Eisenhower called for Hawaii to be admitted as a state but intentionally omitted Alaska from his State of the Union address. Once again, national politics were at play, as it was thought that Hawaii would vote Republican while Alaska would side with the Democrats. Since the Republican majority in Congress at that time was slim, any movement toward the Democrats could shift the balance of power in Congress.

Statehood bills continued to be introduced but without success. Some bills proposed statehood status for both Hawaii and Alaska but these also failed to pass. Another bill was submitted that called for both Hawaii and Alaska to be made into U.S. commonwealths, a status considered inferior to statehood.

In 1956, Alaskans overwhelmingly voted on a state constitution, which garnered much national attention and stepped up the pressure on Washington. In the same year, citizens of Alaska voted on two U.S. senators and one U.S. representative to Congress. While these representatives did not receive official recognition in Congress, it served to maintain pressure on the federal government.

This pressure continued to build until 1957 when the official territorial delegate to Congress, Bob Bartlett, managed to sway Sam Rayburn, the powerful Speaker of the House, into holding hearings on Alaskan statehood. That same year, the Eisenhower administration withdrew 20 million North Slope acres from the military exclusion area with the express intent to make the land available for commercial exploitation, including oil and gas leasing. By 1958, even President Eisenhower could not contain the statehood juggernaut, so he finally endorsed a move toward statehood. Congressional support had finally reached the tipping point, and statehood bills were introduced in both the House and Senate. The House version of the bill passed by wide margins in both chambers. On January 3, 1959, President Eisenhower signed the bill, which declared Alaska to be the forty-ninth state, thereby beating Hawaii in the race toward statehood.

Ironically, despite grave concerns that Alaska would vote alongside liberal Democrats, Alaskans have tended to vote for Republicans in the presidential elections, with the sole exception being Lyndon Johnson. Most of the U.S. Senators and congressmen have been Republicans, and the Alaskan state legislature has been dominated by conservative Republicans. It appears that Eisenhower's fears were grossly unfounded.

Chapter III: The Creation of ANWR

THE DIN FROM STATEHOOD celebrations had barely receded when, on December 6, 1960, U.S. Secretary of the Interior Fred Seaton established the Arctic National Wildlife Range (Public Land Order 2214). This act set aside 8.9 million acres "for the purpose of preserving unique wildlife, wilderness and recreational values ... and reserved for the use of the United States Fish and Wildlife Service as the Arctic National Wildlife Range."

Interestingly, this act withdrew the acreage from all forms of appropriation under public laws, including mining, with the critical exception of the mineral leasing laws. Under the U.S. Fish and Wildlife Service, hunting, fishing, and trapping could be permitted. Such was the beginning of what was to become the Arctic National Wildlife Refuge, or ANWR.

Another significant piece of legislation that would greatly impact the current debate was the Alaskan Native Claims Settlement Act (ANCSA), which was enacted by Congress in 1971 (Public Law 92-203). The purpose of this act was to resolve all native aboriginal land claims in Alaska. In addition to financial reimbursement, village corporations were created that granted surface rights to approximately 22 million acres throughout the state. This included surface rights to parts of what was then known as the Arctic National Wildlife Range. It is important to note that only surface rights were initially granted to the village corporations, while subsurface mineral rights were specifically excluded and remained in control of the federal government.

The Alaskan Native Claims Settlement Act also established Arctic Slope regional corporations, which could obtain subsurface rights to some lands and full title to others. However, subsurface rights on all National Wildlife Ranges in Alaska were not available at the onset.

The Kaktovik Inupiat Corporation (KIC) was one such village corporation that was formed and situated within ANWR. KIC received surface rights to three townships along the coastal plain of ANWR. However, in a subsequent 1983 land swap, subsurface rights to 94,000 acres in the KIC area were transferred from the U.S. government to the Arctic Slope Regional Corporation (ASRC).

The Alaskan Native Claims Settlement Act, the regional corporations, and the Kaktovik Inupiat Corporation would eventually exert a profound influence in the debate over whether to open ANWR for mineral leasing.

In 1967, oil was discovered west of ANWR at Prudhoe Bay on the coastal plain of Alaska's North Slope. With recoverable oil reserves approaching 14 billion barrels of oil (BBO), this discovery would forever alter the economic, social, and political landscape for Alaskans (more on this in a later chapter).

On December 2, 1980, Public Law 96-487 was approved. Known as the Alaska National Interest Lands Conservation Act of 1980 (ANILCA), it greatly expanded federal ownership over land in Alaska by designating certain properties as national parks, national forests, national wildlife refuges, and wild and scenic rivers. All together, ANILCA created 79.54 million acres of refuges in Alaska, of which 24.47 million acres received a Wilderness designation.

ANILCA also added 9.1 million acres to the existing 8.9 million acres in ANWR, expanding it to the south and southwest. An additional 1.3 million acres of state land was added in 1983, bringing the total area for ANWR to 19.3 million acres. ANILCA also officially changed the name from "Arctic National Wildlife Range" to "Arctic National Wildlife Refuge."

Section 1002 of ANILCA addressed the possibility of mineral leasing on the coastal plain of ANWR, now referred to as the "1002 Area" of ANWR. The act called for a study of the natural resource potential of the 1002 Area to be completed and submitted to Congress within five years and nine months of the act's enactment. Specifically, the secretary of the interior was directed to:

> conduct biological and geological studies of the 1.5 million acre coastal plain of the Arctic National Wildlife Refuge (the 1002 Area), report the results of those studies to the Congress, and recommend to Congress

whether the 1002 Area should be made available for oil and gas exploration and development.

Section 1003 of ANILCA prohibited leasing of mineral rights in the 1002 Area unless specifically authorized by an act of Congress.

The 1002 Area comprises 1.5 million acres, or 7.8 percent of ANWR. The 1002 Area of the coastal plain is bordered on the north by the Beaufort Sea, on the west by the Canning River, and on the east by the Yukon Territory of Canada.

ANWR continues to be managed by the U.S. Fish and Wildlife Service of the Department of the Interior.

Chapter IV:
The 1002 Area Hydrocarbon Resource Potential

THE FIRST RESOURCE ASSESSMENT of the oil and natural gas potential of the 1002 Area was conducted primarily by the U.S. Geological Survey (USGS) in coordination with the Bureau of Land Management and the Fish and Wildlife Service. In 1987, it was published in the *U.S. Geological Survey Bulletin*, Volume 1778 (edited by Bird and Magoon). This assessment was a fundamental part of the 1987 report and recommendation to Congress.

The initial assessment of oil and gas potential was based "upon data derived from seismic, surface, geological, geochemical, aeromagnetic, gravity, and other studies, as well as subsurface data from contiguous or analog areas." It is critical to note that the largest oil field in North America, the Prudhoe Bay Field, lay just 80 miles to the west and was already in full production by 1987. Hence, data from "contiguous or analog areas" no doubt provided a major component to the study. At one time, production from the Prudhoe Bay complex of associated fields pumped 2 million barrels of oil per day (MMBOPD) into the 800-mile Trans Alaska Pipeline to the southern port of Valdez. Initial reserves of Prudhoe Bay were 10 billion barrels recoverable, but that estimate has since been revised to 14 billion barrels of oil. A barrel of oil contains forty-two gallons.

Because of the many variables in determining how much oil and gas may exist in the 1002 Area, the USGS could not assign a specific number to resource estimates. Instead, the assessment assigned risks and probabilities to the various hydrocarbon prospects. Based on the limited data available to them, the USGS were able to identify twenty-six hydrocarbon prospects and assign values to them. Reserves were then calculated for each prospect. The range of in-place oil and gas resources were then plotted as a cumulative probability distribution, with the larger quantities of hydrocarbon resources corresponding to lower probabilities of occurrence. In 1987, USGS reported the resource potential of the 1002 Area at the 95th, 5th, and "mean" percentile on the cumulative probability distribution curve as follows:

	95%	5%	Mean
Oil in-place (in BBO)	4.8	29.4	13.8
Gas in-place (in TCF)	11.5	64.5	31.3

BBO = billion barrels of oil
TCF = trillion cubic feet of gas

The arithmetic mean is obtained by taking the sum of all the values on the probability distribution curve and dividing by the number of values. Hence, it is an average of all the points on the curve, not just the average of the 5th and 95th percentile. The arithmetic mean is generally the number most commonly used when discussing the resource potential of ANWR.

The USGS conducted an earlier hydrocarbon resource assessment in 1980, with dramatically different results. The 1980 report estimated mean oil in-place to be 4.9 BBO, and mean gas in-place to be 11.9 TCF. It is believed that the earlier figures understated the resource potential for several technical reasons, one of which was the failure to stack potential reservoirs in a given prospect. This factor alone could have a profound impact on resource estimates. It is also important to state that the above estimates are only a scientific best guess, given the existing data, in the absence of actual field discoveries. Once exploratory drilling takes place, these resource estimates could change dramatically, in either direction.

It is critical to note that the above numbers only reflect "in-place" oil and gas resource potential: that is, oil and gas that is in the ground and not yet extracted by conventional means. Estimates of "recoverable reserves" are less than the in-place reserves because not all the oil and gas can be extracted from the subsurface. Recoverable reserves only refer to those reserves that can be extracted from the subsurface using all known technical recovery techniques. Neither the price per barrel of oil nor the cost of recovering the oil are factors at this point.

Commercially recoverable reserves are generally what is understood when reserves are discussed in a public forum. Hence, production and transportation costs, annual operating expenses, taxes, royalties, and ultimately the price of a barrel of oil are the primary factors in determining if reserves are commercially viable. Many a discovery has been made where the cost to produce the oil exceeded the revenues from that production, thus rendering the discovery non-commercial.

The 1987 USGS report calculated the minimum commercial field size for the 1002 Area to be 440 million barrels of oil. That is, only prospects whose size might yield recoverable reserves of 440 MMBO or greater were deemed to be economically viable. Only eighteen of the twenty-six prospects identified by the USGS met these criteria. The costs of operating on Alaska's North Slope under highly remote and extreme environmental conditions contribute greatly to the magnitude of this number. Most oil companies base their minimum commercial field size on whether they would obtain a sufficient present value and rate of return that is commensurate with the risk. Otherwise, it would be safer for them to invest their capital in Treasury bills or other low-risk investments. Many wildcat exploratory wells are only given a 10 percent chance of success.

No value was assigned to a minimum commercial field size for natural gas in the 1002 Area because it was assumed that natural gas would either not be developed or only used locally in minimal quantities. This could change in the future once a transportation system is developed and a viable market is established for natural gas from both the 1002 Area and the already proven gas reserves at Prudhoe Bay.

In 1998, the USGS revised upward their estimate of the hydrocarbon resources in the 1002 Area as follows:

	95%	5%	Mean
Oil in-place (in BBO)	11.6	31.5	20.7

BBO = billion barrels of oil

The new estimates contrast markedly with the 1987 report, which calculated mean oil-in-place of 13.8 BBO.

19

The 1998 report also calculated technically recoverable reserves in the range of 4.3 to 11.8 BBO, with mean recoverable reserves of 7.7 BBO. Technically recoverable reserves represent 37 percent of the estimated in-place oil reserves. The 1998 study was expanded to include not only the federal 1002 Area, but also the native lands and adjacent state waters. *The combined recoverable reserves of these three areas were 10.4 BBO, with the federal 1002 Area containing 74 percent of those reserves.*

So what transpired from 1987 to 1998 that would warrant such a dramatic increase in resource estimates? Put simply, more data became available, along with better methods of interpreting that data. Approximately twenty new wells were drilled to the west and offshore ANWR that shed new light on the potential of the 1002 Area. In addition, existing data, including seismic, was reprocessed and reinterpreted in light of advanced theories regarding hydrocarbon generation, migration, and entrapment. Finally, this data was integrated with the known petroleum discoveries in both northern Alaska and Canada's Mackenzie Delta.

Rather than identify individual prospects, as was done in the 1987 assessment, the USGS instead focused on ten hydrocarbon plays that corresponded to similar plays on trend to the east and west of ANWR. A hydrocarbon "play" can be defined as a trend in which prospects of similar geologic and geographic characteristics exist. For example, sandstone reservoirs of a certain age range that were deposited in a similar environment and subject to the same burial, migration, and trapping conditions would constitute a play. Within that play would be multiple prospects. Plays can overlap each other, thus allowing for multiple reservoirs to be stacked in a single prospect.

A March 2005 article by petroleum consultant Scott L. Montgomery in the *American Association of Petroleum Geologists Bulletin* states that, to the west of ANWR, there have been thirty-seven discoveries on the North Slope of Alaska, with approximate recoverable reserves of 19 BBO and 46 TCF. To the east of ANWR, Canada's Mackenzie Delta has yielded forty-eight discoveries, with approximate recoverable reserves of 2 BBO and 12 TCF gas. Hence, ANWR's Section 1002 resource estimate of 7.7 BBO recoverable (10.4 BBO including native lands and state offshore out to three miles) falls somewhere between the North Slope and Mackenzie Delta actual reserves.

In essence, the 1998 USGS resource assessment can be considered a more accurate picture of the hydrocarbon potential of the 1002 Area. However, one needs to be reminded that, until exploratory wells are actually drilled in the 1002 Area, the above estimates remain a scientific best guess.

Various attempts have been made to quantify the economic viability of the resource estimates of the 1002 Area. One can assume that every energy company interested in exploring this area will have conducted its own proprietary economic analyses. E. D. Attanasi of the USGS published an economic update in 2005. Adjusted for 2003 dollars, this update showed that, at $30 per barrel, approximately 73 percent to 82 percent of the recoverable reserves were economically viable. At $55 per barrel (in 2003 dollars), greater than 90 percent of the reserves were deemed to be economic. While these numbers would have to be adjusted to more current dollar values, they clearly indicate that a majority of the resources in the 1002 Area are commercially attractive so long as the price of oil remains at its historic high levels of the past few years. And if history can serve as our guide, technological improvements in exploring, drilling, and producing oil will continue to offset other costs associated with operating in an extreme environment.

What assumptions were made in conducting the above economic analysis?

Attanasi assumed that field development techniques would include conventional horizontal and multilateral drilling, thereby reducing the number and size of drill pads required. Gravel drill pads would contain as many as forty wellheads, contrasting sharply with early production at Prudhoe Bay, which only allowed one well per pad. Hence, the footprints for the 1002 Area would be substantially reduced.

Exploration activity, including seismic, wildcat drilling, and temporary roads and airstrips, normally occurs during the winter months on the North Slope, when ice roads and drill pads can be constructed, leaving little trace in the spring when the ice melts. More permanent gravel drill pads are required, however, for development wells and production facilities. Attanasi incorporated a 30 percent premium on exploration and production costs in the 1002 Area as compared to similar activities on the North Slope, primarily due to the remoteness of the area and corresponding lack of infrastructure. It was assumed that the first twenty wildcat wells drilled in Area 1002 would cost a minimum of $15 million (in 2003 dollars), roughly twice that of the development wells.

A 12 percent after-tax rate of return on investment was used to set the standard for economic viability. This is consistent with the practice of many energy companies, although some companies may set a 10 percent rate of return as their economic hurdle. Absent from the USGS analysis is an assumption as to what bonus payments might be paid by energy companies to the federal government for leases in the 1002 Area. These could be substantial but are also very difficult to quantify. The analysis did, however, incorporate state and federal taxes and royalties, as well as the cost to explore, drill, develop, produce, process, and transport the oil to market. Natural gas development was briefly considered but was determined to be too speculative at the time, given that approximately 46 TCF of natural gas has already been discovered on Alaska's North Slope, and a viable market has yet to be established. Any natural gas associated with oil production would initially be re-injected in order to maintain reservoir pressure and boost production rates.

The USGS 2005 analysis envisaged two development scenarios: Scenario One assumed that most field discoveries, with the exception of the smallest, would be developed on a stand-alone basis, with their own field processing facilities. Scenario Two presumed that the fields would send their oil, and associated fluids, to a central processing facility. Under Scenario Two, there would be two central processing areas, one immediately to the west of Area 1002, and another within the native lands component of Area 1002. Most of the oil, approximately 80 percent, would fall within the western part of 1002 and therefore would be processed at the western facility.

Under both scenarios, the oil would be transported via a regional line to Pump Station #1 of the Trans Alaska Pipeline System. TAPS currently transports less than 1 MMBO daily from the North Slope fields a distance of 800 miles to the port of Valdez in southern Alaska. From there, the oil is transferred to tankers and delivered to markets on the U.S. West Coast and elsewhere. In its heyday (1988), TAPS was pumping 2 MMBO daily. Thus, it has the capacity to accommodate at least 1 MMBO from Area 1002 fields.

The distance from TAPS Pump Station #1 to the proposed western central processing facility is eighty-five miles. It would be another fifty miles to reach the eastern processing facility. Regional pipelines with a diameter capable of transporting 500,000 BOPD to Pump Station #1 were assumed. Larger diameter pipelines, while initially more costly, would have the distinct advantage of increased carrying capacity and could therefore accommodate new field discoveries. Given the resource estimates for Area 1002, and the volumes of oil historically produced from North Slope fields, it would not be unreasonable to contemplate achieving cumulative production rates of 1 MMBOPD.

While the above economic analysis reflects that of the USGS, interested energy companies have also made their own economic assessments (which would be considered proprietary and therefore not in the public domain). Despite the multiple variables involved and the sensitivity to oil pricing, the USGS study demonstrates a knowledgeable and comprehensive approach toward establishing the viability of oil exploration and development in the 1002 Area.

Chapter V: ANWR Comprehensive Conservation Plan and Environmental Impact Statement

IN ACCORDANCE WITH THE Alaska National Interest Lands Conservation Act of 1980 and the Environmental Policy Act of 1969, the U.S. Fish and Wildlife Service produced the "Final Comprehensive Conservation Plan and Environmental Impact Statement" for ANWR in 1988. Although this voluminous report included the Section 1002 Area of the Arctic coastal plain, it specifically did not address the impact of hydrocarbon leasing in ANWR. The reason given was that oil and gas leasing was prohibited in the 1002 Area unless specifically authorized by Congress. Instead, this thorny issue was covered in a separate report, referred to as the "Section 1002h Report and Legislative Environmental Impact Statement," submitted to Congress in June 1987 by the secretary of the interior.

The secretary's 1987 report to Congress addressed five alternatives for future management of the 1002 Area of the Arctic coastal plain. These are as follows:

A. Congressional authorization to lease the entire 1002 Area for hydrocarbon exploration and development.

B. Congressional authorization to lease part of the 1002 Area for hydrocarbon exploration and development, with the exclusion of the upper Jago River area.

C. Allow additional exploration before congressional authority for leasing is granted.

D. Continue to manage the 1002 Area under the U.S. Fish and

Wildlife Comprehensive Conservation Plan, with no action required by Congress. Hence, no leasing would be allowed.

E. Designate the entire 1002 Area as a "Wilderness Area", in accordance with the 1964 Wilderness Act. Therefore, no commercial activity of any kind would be allowed.

Secretary of Interior Hodel strongly endorsed Alternative A, which called upon Congress to enact legislation that would open the entire 1.5 MM acre 1002 Area for hydrocarbon exploration and development. Rather than discuss each alternative scenario in detail, it would be best to focus on the secretary's recommendation to Congress, the reasons given for putting forth that recommendation, and the subsequent rejection of that proposal by Congress.

Secretary Hodel essentially stressed that prudent development of the 1002 Area would yield substantial economic benefits and enhance the energy security of the nation while simultaneously mitigating any environmental impact on the area.

He argued against a Wilderness designation on the basis that the 1002 Area was not unique and that Alaska already had 55 million acres set aside as Wilderness, and another 80 million acres designated as national parks, preserves, wildlife refuges, and wild and scenic rivers. In addition, ANWR is bordered on the east by the 3 million acre Northern Yukon National Park of Canada.

Regarding the effect of development on fish and wildlife species, the secretary stated:

> The fish and wildlife species that might be affected by oil and gas activities in the 1002 Area are very important but are neither threatened nor endangered. In fact, they are relatively abundant in Alaska and North America.

Secretary Hodel then went on to report that:

> the Porcupine caribou herd is the sixth largest caribou herd in North America. The musk-ox reintroduction has been so successful that some hunting is now permitted.

The potential impact on subsistence by native Alaskans was also addressed in the report to Congress. The secretary discussed both the impact on the village of Kaktovik, located inside the 1002 Area, and the impact of native villages "far removed" from the area. The impact on villages outside the 1002 Area, including those in the Canadian Yukon, was considered to be minimal. Migration patterns of the Porcupine caribou would also be unaffected by exploration and development activities. In essence, no change.

In Kaktovik, however, the secretary envisioned the potential for a "major restriction of subsistence activities." This would no doubt be an indirect result of exploration activities in the 1002 Area and a direct result of development facilities being located on or adjacent to the village lands. Wildlife migration patterns would be altered in the immediate vicinity. Secretary Hodel stated that the Department of the Interior would work with the village of Kaktovik to minimize this impact.

At this juncture, the author would interject several points:

The first is that the comments by the secretary of the interior to the Congress are not entirely consistent with the U.S. Fish and Wildlife "Comprehensive Conservation Plan and Environmental Impact Statement," particularly with respect to the impact on wildlife and migration patterns. In addition, the impact on neighboring native villages outside the 1002 Area, with respect to subsistence living, may have been understated. Canada would take strong exception to Secretary Hodel's remarks. At the same time, the impact on Kaktovik, although potentially significant, may not necessarily be a bad thing in the eyes of the villagers (more on these topics later). Giving Secretary Hodel the benefit of the doubt, he may have been attempting to boil down a massively complex set of issues to a few salient points for the benefit of a Congress with a short attention span, while at the same time putting forward the administration's best argument for leasing.

One can only assume that the secretary put forward Alternatives B (limited leasing) and C (exploration only) in the event that open leasing of the entire 1002 Area (Alternative A) met with stiff resistance in Congress. While energy companies would want to conduct further exploration in an effort to more precisely determine the hydrocarbon potential of the area, they would be reluctant to expend vast sums of capital unless there was some assurance that the area would eventually become available for leasing. Absent such an assurance, shareholders would not look kindly on such expenditures. Limited leasing, which excludes the upper Jago River area, is postulated to reduce the oil resource estimate by 25 percent, with a projected 30 percent decline in the mean expected economic benefit to the nation. The primary reason for excluding the upper Jago River is stated to be the risk to the Porcupine caribou herd. Limited leasing is not a bad fallback position. It mitigates the impact on the caribou and still provides enough incentive for energy companies to pursue leases in the remaining area.

In the end, Congress took no action.

The ANWR "Comprehensive Conservation Plan and Environmental Impact Statement" (EIS) conducted by the U.S. Fish and Wildlife Service presents a somewhat different picture of the impact of hydrocarbon leasing in the 1002 Area. The service identified ten "potential management concerns" for ANWR. Several of these concerns are related to increased public use, fishing, hunting, and conflicts between users. Four of these concerns relate directly to hydrocarbon exploration and production, and mining. These concerns are as follows:

1   Oil and gas exploration and development on Refuge lands

2   Mining within the Refuge

3   Development and use of adjacent lands

4   Private inholdings within the Refuge boundary

Oil and Gas Exploration and Development on Refuge Lands

The EIS stated that problems with wildlife, habitats, and marine life would occur should Congress allow hydrocarbon exploration and development to take place in the 1002 Area. Specifically, there would be displacement of wildlife where facilities would be constructed, particularly with regard to the Porcupine caribou herd. In addition, there would be loss of habitat due to construction of facilities, roads, pipelines, and airstrips, and increased public usage. A "potential major impact" is envisioned should there be displacement of the Porcupine caribou herd from their traditional calving grounds. In addition, the musk-ox could be similarly impacted, with a subsequent reduction in the herd's growth rate.

Related to the above implications for wildlife habitat, air and water quality are anticipated to be diminished in the vicinity of any large-scale production facilities. Detrimental emissions from production facilities include black smoke, carbon monoxide, sulfuric and nitric oxides, and heavy metals. Fresh water is stated to be in limited supply on the coastal plain, and the availability and usage would need to be properly assessed prior to any consideration for facilities development.

Mining within the Refuge

Apparently, there are existing mining claims but no significant ongoing mining operations in ANWR. Mining on or near the coastal plain would essentially take the form of gravel mining, which is used primarily for road construction. In the event of exploration and production operations, gravel may also be used for constructing roads, airstrips, and pads for exploration and production facilities. According to the EIS, the negative impact from gravel mining is not so much a result of the mining itself, but of the problems that would result from greater human access to ANWR:

"If a permanent road was necessary into the developed area it could result in increased human presence, which could reduce certain fish and wildlife populations using these lands and waters."

One could argue that any increased human activity, whether it occurred from oil operations, or tourism, or mining, or hunting and fishing, would have such a potential detrimental impact on fish and wildlife. Hence, this goes to the heart of the issue as to whether ANWR should be open for any purpose, not just oil and gas leasing.

Development and Use of Adjacent Lands

Lands adjacent to ANWR are under the control of various federal, state, native, private, and foreign (Canada) agencies or corporations. Since fish and wildlife migration patterns do not adhere to political boundaries, many species migrate between ANWR and adjoining lands and waterways. This would include caribou, bears, and wolves. Hence, any development activities that occur on adjacent lands could have a profound, adverse impact on ANWR.

According to the EIS:

> Impacts may include loss and/or alteration of terrestrial and aquatic habitats, increased pollution and littering, introduction of non-native species, and increased human use of available resources.

The EIS makes particular mention of the offshore area of the ANWR coastal plain. State waters extend from the shoreline, defined as submerged tidal lands, out to three miles. Beyond the three-mile limit, the federal government maintains jurisdiction. The federal Minerals Management Service (MMS) manages offshore oil and gas leasing and operations for the U.S. government. The tidal lagoons on the coastal plain have been the subject of a dispute between the state and the MMS, but no leasing of the lagoonal areas by the state will take place until the matter is resolved. In state waters, however, leasing has occurred offshore the ANWR coastal plain and the 1002 Area.

The environmental impact statement recognizes the potential impact from offshore development. Facilities that support offshore operations could conceivably be built onshore ANWR. This has already been addressed in a prior section. In addition, accidental oil spills or pollution from routine offshore operations could detrimentally impact fish and coastal wildlife habitats, including nesting areas for waterfowl.

Although hydrocarbon development of adjacent state lands is deemed to have less of an impact than offshore development, any large-scale development is perceived to have a significant affect on air and water quality and migratory wildlife in ANWR.

Private Inholdings within the Refuge Boundary

There are multiple native-owned lands, allotments, and native corporation lands that are situated within ANWR, totaling approximately 294,000 acres, that have been or will be conveyed. The most significant of these native lands is the village of Kaktovik, which is located within the 1002 Area and comprises approximately 69,000 acres.

The Kaktovik Inupiat Corporation (KIC) owns the surface rights to the village, and the Arctic Slope Regional Corporation (ASRC) owns the mineral, or subsurface, rights. However, under a separate agreement referred to as the Chandler Lake Land Exchange Agreement, ASRC cannot allow oil or gas production to occur unless so authorized by Congress. This would have to be done in conjunction with a similar congressional authorization to open the 1002 Area for leasing. Limited mining operations, specifically gravel mining, have been allowed to take place. The environmental impact from the limited mining operations is deemed to be minimal.

Most of the native allotments are small in size, no more than 160 acres, and are dispersed throughout the Refuge. All together, these allotments would total about 15,000 acres. The biggest concern raised with the allotments, should development occur, would be public trespass.

Another regional native corporation, Doyon, Ltd., has obtained approximately 112,000 acres through conveyance under the Alaska Native Claims Settlement Act. However, these lands are situated on the southern part of the Refuge, well outside the 1002 Area.

Chapter VI: Environmental Considerations

MUCH OF THE INFORMATION in this chapter on environmental considerations is derived from the U.S. Fish and Wildlife "Comprehensive Conservation Plan and Environmental Impact Statement" for the Arctic National Wildlife Refuge, published in 1988.

Ecology

ANWR is considered somewhat unique in that it provides for a broad range of ecosystems within a relatively short distance. Within the short span of 150 miles, one encounters both arctic and subarctic ecosystems, encompassing coastal and mountain (Brooks Range) terrain and habitats. According to the U.S. Fish and Wildlife report:

> The Refuge supports a full complement of arctic flora and fauna, including arctic grayling, arctic char, whitefish, salmon, brown and black bear, Dall sheep, bald and golden eagles, caribou, peregrine falcon, polar bear, musk-ox, moose, wolf, wolverine, and other species of interest to many Americans.

The report further stated that the winter range and a substantial portion of the calving area for the Porcupine caribou herd are included in this system. This particular reference to the plight of the Porcupine caribou is somewhat critical to the environmental factors that have been brought to bear on whether ANWR is opened to development. A more thorough analysis will follow later in this chapter and beyond.

Additionally, the successful reintroduction of the musk-ox has transpired in this area. At a minimum, 400 musk-ox have been identified as ranging along the coastal plain of ANWR.

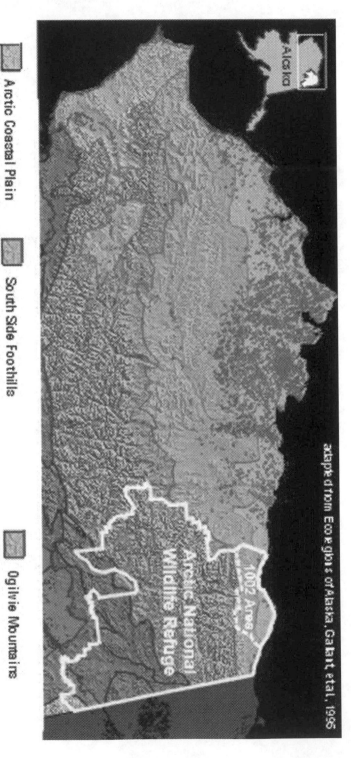

Regional ecosystem map of northern Alaska, courtesy of USFWS

Nine sites within ANWR were described as having special ecological values. Of those nine, the one most germane to the debate is the Beaufort Lagoon-Icy Reef-Kongakut River. The coastal lagoon and offshore bar system are considered noteworthy as arctic lowland geomorphologic features. In addition to the geomorphology, the coastal lagoon system provides habitat support for several species of fish, waterfowl, seals, several species of geese, caribou, musk-ox, wolf, arctic fox, brown bear, peregrine falcon, and gyrfalcon. Included in this system is the lower Kongakut River, as it is considered integral to the coastal lagoon environment.

Climate

Since ANWR encompasses both an arctic coastal and a subarctic mountainous regime, the climate is equally as diverse. As the emphasis here is on the 1002 Area along the coastal plain, the discussion will focus on the climate north of the Brooks Range. North of the Brooks Range, the climate is classified as arctic. No surprise here, as all of ANWR is north of the Arctic Circle. The coastal plain is generally cold to very cold, cloudy, and subject to high winds. July temperatures average forty-one degrees Fahrenheit (five degrees Celsius). February temperatures average four degrees below zero Fahrenheit (twenty degrees below zero Celsius). Extreme lows of forty degrees below zero Fahrenheit (forty degrees below zero Celsius) have been recorded.

Being north of the Arctic Circle, there are days when the sun is continuously either above or below the horizon. This is accentuated in the most northerly portions of the coastal plain, such as Barter Island, where the sun is below the horizon from November 24 to January 17, a total of fifty-five days. At these times, only twilight and moonlight provide a modest source of light. This is in sharp contrast to the summer months, when the sun can be continuously above the horizon at Barter Island from May 15 until July 27.

The prevailing wind direction is from the northeast, with average speeds of 9 to 15 miles (15 to 25 kilometers) per hour. Calm conditions rarely exist, with Barter Island reporting calm winds a mere 4 percent of the time. On occasion, storms arising from the west produce very high winds, on the order of 70 MPH (115 KPH). The windy conditions along the coast contribute to a wind chill factor well below the average temperatures reported above.

Precipitation along the coastal plain is scant, less than 10 inches (25 centimeters) per year of equivalent water. This includes annual snowfall amounts that range from 12 to 47 inches (30 to 119 centimeters). Most of the precipitation occurs as rain during the summer months. Since the rate of evaporation under these climatic conditions is very low, soils tend to remain saturated during the summer.

Air and Water Quality

Given that there is currently little human intervention in ANWR, save for native villages, and subsistence and sport hunting and fishing, both air and water quality are generally regarded as very good. Occasional arctic haze has been detected on the North Slope, which may be due to either natural climatic conditions or airborne pollutants from as far away as Russia.

Geology of the North Slope

For the sake of brevity, one must sacrifice a comprehensive discussion of the complex geology of the North Slope. Instead, the focus will be on those elements that bear on the central issues of this study. The U.S. Fish and Wildlife Service ascribed geological and paleontological values to the ANWR coastal area, specifically the Beaufort Lagoon-Icy Reef-Kongakut River. However, this was purely in the context of whether it fit the criteria for a Wilderness designation.

The surface geology of ANWR North Slope is arctic tundra coastal plain, containing several rivers that flow in a northerly direction toward the sea. The three major terrain types in the 1002 Area are classified as foothills (45 percent), river floodplains (25 percent), hilly coastal plain (22 percent), and other lesser terrain types (8 percent). Soils along the coastal plain are primarily derived from fluvial sand and silt, with marine sediments along the shore.

Much of the surface of ANWR is permafrost, where the soil deposits are continuously below freezing for at least two years. The depth of permafrost in ANWR's North Slope is considered to be on the order of 1,000 feet (300 meters), with summer thawing limited to no more than 18 inches (46 centimeters). Those lakes along the coastal plain with a depth of greater than 7 feet (2 meters) are usually ice free, as are the deeper parts of rivers.

As to the question of whether ANWR, and more specifically, the 1002 Area, have the requisite geologic elements to produce hydrocarbons, one only needs to look west along the coast, to where the Prudhoe Bay complex of fields currently produce. To the east, there is the McKenzie River Delta field complex. The 1002 Area sits between these field complexes and directly on trend. The same lithologic and structural elements apply. The source rocks, burial history, reservoir rocks, and trapping mechanisms are essentially the same. According to S. L. Montgomery.:

> Most or all units productive of oil at Prudhoe Bay and oil and gas bearing strata in the Mackenzie Delta region are present in the 1002 Area. Most of the hydrocarbon resources in the 1002 Area have both its source and reservoir in Upper Cretaceous-Tertiary (Brookian) strata. These strata were developed in a foreland basin that developed in front (north) of the evolving Brooks Range thrust-fold orogen.

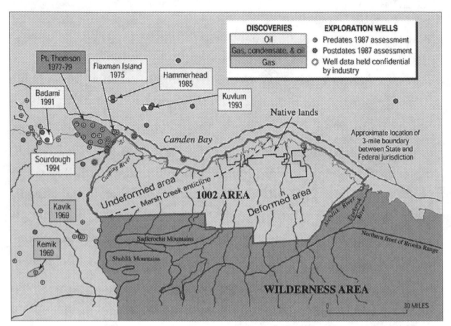

Hydrocarbon discoveries in close proximity to ANWR, courtesy of USGS

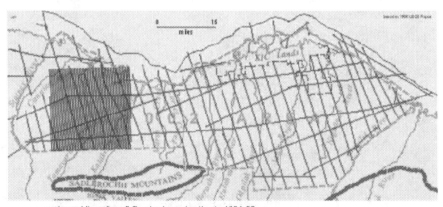

Seismic lines across ANWR, courtesy of USGS

This information is primarily based on the limited seismic data and field studies that were conducted in ANWR during the 1980s. The USGS reports, as previously mentioned, detailed the number of play types and prospects, and potential reserves in the 1002 Area.

Vegetation

The USGS and the U.S. Fish and Wildlife Service identified twenty-three types of land cover vegetation for ANWR. This was accomplished mostly through the employment of Landsat imagery. The 1002 Area contains mostly scarcely vegetated or barren floodplain along the northerly flowing rivers and streams, set amid a predominantly wet tundra complex over the permafrost substrate. It is mostly treeless and supports low shrubs, moss, lichen, and peaty soils. The tundra soil group is characterized by very poor drainage, with an organically rich upper layer.

ANWR coastal plain: photo courtesy of USGS

Fish and Wildlife

The U.S. Fish and Wildlife Service identified 249 species of vertebrates that either inhabit or migrate through the Arctic National Wildlife Refuge. This consists of 36 kinds of fish, 169 birds, 8 marine mammals, and 36 terrestrial mammals. Brevity precludes addressing each individual species in this report, but the more significant species and those more likely to be impacted by development will be discussed.

Fish

Of the thirty-six species of fish found in and along the coast of ANWR, none are reported to be harvested commercially in the immediate area. The nearest commercial fishery is west of ANWR in the Colville River, where arctic cisco is harvested. Some fish are taken by Kaktovik residents as part of their subsistence living. These are predominantly arctic char, arctic and least cisco, salmon, arctic grayling, arctic cod, and four-horn sculpin.

Many of the saltwater fish species spawn in brackish to freshwater rivers and streams along the coast. While migration patterns of the fish might not be heavily impacted by onshore development, any activity that would disturb the rivers, streams, and coastal lagoons during spawning season could have some impact. Quantifying such an impact on a migratory species of fish could prove challenging, and would most likely necessitate annual counts over a number of years. Although most exploration operations, including seismic and drilling, occur during the winter months when spawning activities are low, ongoing production operations, including pipelines and roads, need to consider the potential impact on spawning areas.

Birds

At least 169 species of birds inhabit ANWR, with 108 identified on the North Slope. In addition, migratory birds from lands as distant as Antarctica (arctic terns), South America (golden plovers, buff-breasted sandpipers), and Asia and Africa (yellow wagtails, bluethroats) are seen in ANWR. Tundra swans and snow geese nest along the Arctic coastal plain. Several species of ducks also nest in the lagoons and tundra lakes. Subsistence hunting of ducks and geese occurs to a limited extent. Seabirds such as jaegers, artic tern, and black guillemots also breed on the coastal plain. Shorebirds such as sandpipers and sandhill cranes are also known to nest along the coastal plain.

Numerous other birds inhabit the southern part of ANWR, in the foothills and mountainous Brooks Range, including nineteen species of raptors. The raptors include the American peregrine falcon, which is on the endangered species list, and the arctic peregrine falcon, which is classified as a threatened species. The American peregrine falcon is found on ANWR's southern boundary (south of the Brooks Range) and would not fall within the 1002 Area. Hence, it would not be impacted by oil and gas operations. However, the threatened arctic peregrine falcon is found on the North Slope and might be impacted. The arctic peregrine falcons have been observed to both nest and migrate along the Arctic coastal plain, where shorebirds are their likely prey.

Marine Mammals

Marine mammals offshore ANWR include the polar bear, ringed and bearded seals, and bowhead and beluga whales. These mammals are found either along the shore or in the deeper waters offshore. The bowhead whales are classified as an endangered species and are found in the waters five to ten miles (eight to sixteen kilometers) offshore the Refuge in the spring and fall when they migrate from the Beaufort to the Bering Sea. Despite their classification as an endangered species, the bowhead whales are considered a major staple of the Kaktovik people, and subsistence hunting is allowed under the Endangered Species Act. Estimates place the population of bowheads in the range of 2,000 to 4,000. Given their distance from shore, any onshore development in the 1002 Area is not likely to impact the whales. However, offshore development and shipping could disturb the feeding and migration patterns of the whales.

Polar bears pose another concern. These mammals generally are associated with sea ice in the Arctic Ocean, which constitutes their primary seal feeding grounds. While most polar bear dens are situated offshore on the sea ice, some females will come ashore to give birth to cubs, and a number of den sites have been confirmed within the ANWR coastal plain by the U.S. Fish and Wildlife Service. Polar bear den sites have been observed 250 miles offshore (400 kilometers) and 32 miles inland (51 kilometers). Within ANWR's coastal plain, a total of eight den sites were found during the early to mid-1980s. After the cubs are born (December to January), they will generally move out to the sea ice in March or April.

Mother polar bear and cubs

The total polar bear population in the circumpolar arctic region is estimated at 20,000 to 25,000. However, the bear population is experiencing a serious decline that is believed to be due to decreasing Arctic sea ice. According to the U.S. Department of the Interior, the sea ice has diminished by anywhere from 7.7 percent per decade since the 1960s to as much as 32 percent in localized areas. The receding sea ice has deprived the bears of much of their hunting grounds for their primary staple, the seals. The receding ice is believed to be a direct result of climate change.

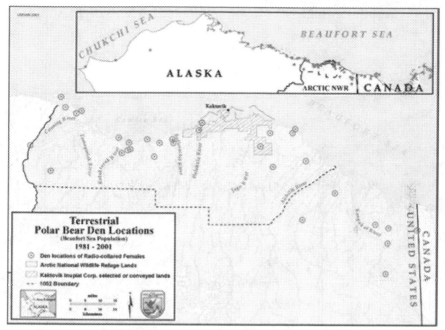

Polar bear den map: courtesy of USFWS

Observations of weight loss in the adult bears and a reduced survival rate among the cubs prompted U.S. Department of the Interior Secretary Kempthorne to propose listing the polar bear as a threatened species under the Endangered Species Act (December 27, 2006). Polar bears are already protected under the Marine Mammal Protection Act of 1972 as well as several international treaties, including the U.S.-Russia Polar Bear Conservation and Management Act.

After considerable debate, on May 14, 2008, the U.S. Department of the Interior listed the polar bear as a threatened species under the Endangered Species Act. A "threatened species" is likely to become an endangered species in the foreseeable future. An "endangered species" is in danger of extinction. In making this determination, Interior Secretary Kempthorne stated the following:

> Today's decision is based on three findings. First, sea ice is vital to polar bear survival. Second, the polar bear's sea-ice habitat has dramatically melted in recent

decades. Third, computer models suggest sea ice is likely to further recede in the future.

The accompanying Department of the Interior news release clarified the listing as it related to economic activities:

> In making the decision to list the polar bear as a threatened species, Kempthorne also announced he was using the authority provided in Section 4(d) of the ESA (Endangered Species Act) to develop a rule that states if an activity is permissible under the stricter standards imposed by the Marine Mammal Protection Act, it is also permissible under the Endangered Species Act with respect to the polar bear. This rule, effective immediately, will ensure the protection of the bear while allowing us to continue to develop our natural resources in the arctic region in an environmentally sound way.

Subsistence hunting of polar bears is still allowed under all of the above legislation and treaties. However, if it is determined that subsistence harvesting materially affects the sustainability of the bear population, the Department of Interior will most likely revisit the viability of such an exemption.

Regarding energy development, Secretary Kempthorne earlier had stated, "The [Fish and Wildlife] Service extensively analyzed the impact of both onshore and offshore oil and gas development on polar bears and determined they do not pose a threat to the species."

Notwithstanding this assurance from Secretary Kempthorne, it would seem prudent to take into consideration the preservation of any known denning areas within the refuge.

Terrestrial Mammals

Despite the seemingly barren landscape, thirty-six species of terrestrial mammals are known to co-exist within ANWR. These include moose, caribou, musk-oxen, Dall sheep, black and brown bears, wolves, wolverines, and smaller mammals. While many of these mammals are hunted both for sport and subsistence purposes, none are classified as threatened or endangered. Many of these mammals inhabit areas well to the south of the 1002 Area. While all are important, it is not the intent of this book to address every species in detail. However, some deserve special mention.

The musk-oxen in Alaska were wiped out in the 1800s, but were successfully reintroduced on the North Slope in 1969–1970. The herds grew by 26 percent annually, and 476 musk-oxen were counted in a 1985 census. These creatures are not migratory and are generally found foraging for willows along rivers and drainage areas within the coastal plain of the Refuge. While they have natural predators such as wolves and brown bears, the herd is viable to the point where sport hunting of musk-oxen has been allowed since 1983. Since most exploration activities (seismic and drilling) occur during the winter months (when the musk-oxen are most sedentary), care would have to be taken to avoid disturbing known habitat sites.

Musk Oxen in the Snow

In his 1987 recommendation to Congress, Secretary of the Interior Hodel very briefly addressed the musk-oxen issue:

> Musk-oxen disappeared from the 1002 Area at the turn of the century. Those that now occupy the area are the result of a successful reintroduction program. The potential effects of oil and gas activities on the area's musk-oxen are unknown, although biologists predict that "major" effects could be: (1) substantial displacement from currently used habitat and (2) a slowing of the herd's growth rate, as distinguished from a diminution in herd size.

Two types of barren ground caribou are found on the North Slope and within the refuge: the Central Arctic caribou herd and the Porcupine caribou herd. Despite both being caribou, they are distinctly different in size, range, calving, and migratory patterns.

The Central Arctic herd has been increasing in size and numbered 12,000 to 14,000 in 1985 when the U.S. Fish and Wildlife Service conducted their environmental impact study. The range of the Central Arctic herd extends across the Prudhoe Bay-Kuparuk fields as well as the Trans Alaskan Pipeline System and Dalton Highway. While the herd winters in the mountainous areas, it migrates toward the North Slope and the coastal plain during the calving season in the spring. The coastal plain is favored both for post-calving and for insect relief during the summer months. Both sport and subsistence hunting of the Central Arctic caribou are allowed. The fact that the Central Arctic caribou herd has thrived alongside oil field transportation and development facilities at Prudhoe Bay has often been cited by proponents of development for the 1002 Area.

It has been asserted that the mammal likely to be most impacted by development of the 1002 Area is the Porcupine caribou. The Porcupine caribou breed and migrate along ANWR's coastal plain and are considered highly vulnerable to development. Hence, this issue merits a chapter of its own.

Caribou on the move

Chapter VII: The Porcupine Caribou Herd

THE PORCUPINE CARIBOU HERD was estimated to be as large as 178,000 in 1987 and was reduced to 123,000 in 2001. The caribou range over a very large area that encompasses both Canada and the United States, approximated at 96,100 square miles (249,000 square kilometers). ANWR's coastal plain provides essential calving grounds and migration routes, while the southern part of ANWR contains summer, fall, and winter habitats as well as migration routes.

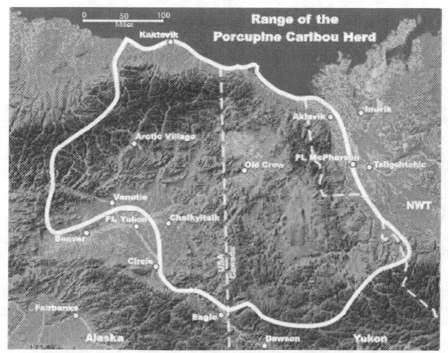

Range of the Porcupine caribou herd: map courtesy of USFWS

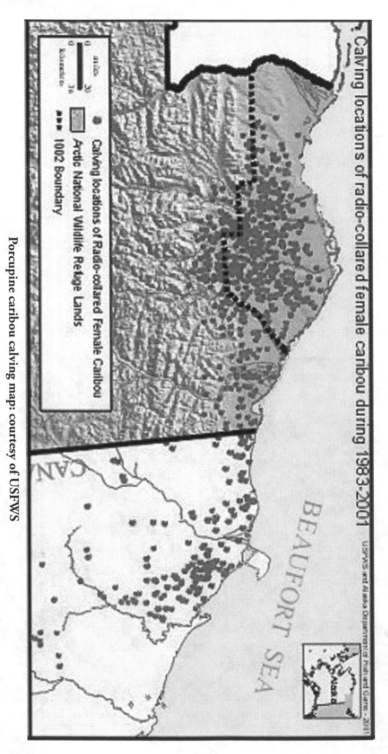

Porcupine caribou calving map: courtesy of USFWS

There appears to be little dispute that the Porcupine caribou would be impacted by development in the 1002 Area. The question is to what extent. Even Interior Secretary Hodel, while recommending development in the 1002 Area in his 1987 report to Congress, acknowledged the potential impact on the Porcupine caribou:

> Potential impacts were assessed at three stages of oil activity: exploration, development drilling, and production. The impact analyses predicted that exploration and development drilling activities would generate only minor or negligible effects on *all* wildlife resources on the 1002 area. The only potential "major" effects are attendant to oil *production* and are limited to the Porcupine caribou herd and the reintroduced musk-ox herd.

After making such a profound statement, the secretary tended to water down its impact with the following pronouncement:

> "Major biological effects," for purposes of this analysis, were defined as widespread, long-term change in habitat availability or quality which would likely modify natural abundance or distribution of species. Modification will persist at least as long as modifying influences exist. Therefore, "major" is not synonymous with adverse. Either of two conditions, change in species distribution *or* population dynamics, would result in a rating of "major."

The caribou are known to calve in several areas, including Canada, along the coastal plain of ANWR, and within the 1002 Area. The calving grounds reportedly encompass an area as large as 8.9 million acres, from the Canning River in Alaska to the Babbage River in Canada. In addition to occupying the 1002 Area during calving season, they also remain there briefly during post-calving and insect relief season. This total time period spans six to eight weeks annually, and occurs from mid-May to mid-July. Peak calving in ANWR occurs during the first week in June. As noted previously, most exploration and drilling activity would transpire during the winter months. However, production facilities within the 1002 Area, including roads and pipelines, would overlap with the presence of the caribou. The caribou have shown a preference for calving in the vicinity of the upper Jago River, a portion of which (5.4 percent) falls within the 1002 Area. If oil field development were to transpire in this area, it is reasonable to anticipate a significant displacement would transpire. This would therefore constitute a "major" effect as defined in the interior secretary's recommendation to Congress.

It has been pointed out that the Central Arctic caribou herd, which calves and ranges through the Prudhoe Bay complex to the west, has tripled in size since oil field development began in the late 1960s. This required adapting to roads and pipelines across the migratory routes. Energy companies are quick to indicate that numerous accommodations were made in road and pipeline design to minimize the impact on the Central Arctic caribou, and it appears this effort succeeded. Skeptics assert that the herd might have sustained higher rates of growth in the absence of oil facilities. Such an assertion would be difficult to prove or disprove. However, the Porcupine herd already transits the Dempster Highway in Canada along its migratory route.

Disturbing the Porcupine caribou during calving season is considered to be potentially harmful to the growth rate of the herd. According to the USFWS environmental impact statement:

> Caribou calves are precocious, being able to stand and nurse within 1 hour after birth, and follow their mothers around within a few hours. The first 24 hours of life are critical, when a behavioral bond is formed between the calf and its mother. Disturbance of maternal groups on the calving grounds may interfere with bond formation and can increase calf mortality.

Likewise, the post-calving and insect relief season is considered sensitive to disturbance, as the calves are very young, and the mothers, having just calved, have low energy reserves. Access to insect relief areas and foraging sites is deemed critical at this time. Segments of the herd move toward either the coast or the mountainous areas for insect relief. By mid-July, the herd generally commences its eastward migration toward the wintering grounds in Canada, although some will re-enter the Wildlife Refuge on their way to the Brooks Range. Roughly one third of the herd winters in Alaska.

Humans have reportedly hunted the caribou as far back as 27,000 years. The Porcupine caribou are harvested in both Alaska and Canada. The annual harvest of the caribou has been estimated at somewhere from 3,000 to 5,000. In Alaska, natives from Kaktovik and Arctic Village both conduct subsistence hunting on the herd.

Of significant note is the fact that the Porcupine caribou herd has experienced a decline in recent years. It has the lowest long-term growth rate, 4.9 percent, of all the Alaskan barren ground caribou. By contrast, the Central Arctic herd has a growth rate of 10.8 percent, and the Teshekpuk Lake herd has a growth rate of 13 percent.

The size of the Porcupine caribou herd peaked in the late 1970s through much of the 1980s, reaching 178,000 in number. Thereafter, the growth rate declined to about 3.6 percent per year from 1989 to 1998, and achieved only 1.5 percent growth from 1998 to 2001. The size of the herd was reported to have been reduced to around 123,000 by 2001. In the last two decades of the twentieth century, the survival rate of the adult female Porcupine caribou was put at 84 percent, while the calf survival rate was estimated to be only 48 percent.

The exact cause of the reduction in the size of the herd is not known, although it is speculated that increased freeze–thaw cycles due to warming temperatures in the Arctic have reduced access to forage areas, along with increased predation.

The Biological Resources Division of the U.S. Geological Survey undertook a comprehensive effort to empirically model the potential impact of oil field development on the Porcupine caribou herd, particularly during the critical six- to eight-week calving, post-calving, and insect relief seasons. A total of seven hypothetical oil development scenarios were evaluated as they affected calf survival rates as a function of displacement distance from facilities. The basic assumptions are that the facilities fall within the calving area and that the herd must be displaced a minimum distance of four kilometers from facilities, roads, and pipelines.

As could be predicted, the calf survival rate decreased with an increase in displacement distance. With a net average displacement ranging from 1.2 to 1.7 kilometers, the result was a decrease in the June calf survival rate of 0.7 percent. When the displacement distance increased from 4.3 to 4.7 kilometers, the calf survival rate fell by 1.1 to 1.2 percent. As the distance increased to 21.6 to 23.9 kilometers, the survival rate diminished by 3.7 to 4.0 percent. Finally, when the displacement was as far as 51.9 kilometers, the calf survival rate decreased 8.2 percent. To the casual observer, these diminished calf survival rates as a function of displaced distance from facilities might seem negligible. Keep in mind, however, that the Porcupine caribou have the lowest growth rate (1.5 percent in 2001), so any resultant diminution of the calf survival rate would have serious implications for the sustainability of the herd.

> The USGS study concluded the following:
> Because the assumptions were conservative, the results were conservative. Substantial (10 to 27 km) displacement of concentrated calving areas and associated annual calving grounds and calving sites of the Porcupine caribou herd is likely to negatively affect calf survival during June. At the upper end of this range of displacement (27 km), recovery of the herd from the current decline would be unlikely. These conclusions are consistent with those found in the 1987 "Final Legislative Environmental Impact Statement" (Clough et al. 1987).
>
> Petroleum development will most likely result in restricting the location of concentrated calving areas, calving sites, and annual calving rounds. Expected effects that could be observed include reduced survival of calves during June, reduced weight and condition of parturient [calf- bearing] females and reduced weight of calves in late June, and, potentially, reduced weight and reduced probability of conception for parturient females in the fall.

STAKEHOLDERS

THE NUMBER OF AFFECTED, or vested, parties in the battle over ANWR are legion. They involve numerous and often conflicting entities within the federal, state, and local governments. They involve other nations, such as Canada and Russia. They most definitely involve certain native Alaskan villages and their regional corporations. And, as can be expected, they involve energy companies, a multitude of environmental/conservation groups, and even sporting associations. One could devote entire treatises to each and every one of these stakeholders. However, the purpose here is to concisely identify the affected parties and to address the relevancy of their concerns. No doubt there will be some interested parties who will not be covered in this section. It is emphasized that their issues and concerns will be appropriately addressed nonetheless and that all issues relating to development within the 1002 Area of ANWR will be fully covered.

Chapter VIII: The Federal Government

Executive Branch

The completion of the "Comprehensive Conservation Plan and Environmental Impact Statement" in 1988 paved the way for Congress to consider legislation to open the 1002 Area for leasing. Numerous attempts were made in the Reagan, Clinton, and Bush administrations to pass a bill that would authorize leasing, but none succeeded. The attempts either failed in the House or Senate or were vetoed by President Clinton.

The administration of George W. Bush (2000–2008) staunchly and persistently recommended that the 1002 Area of ANWR be opened for energy exploration and development. In his last State of the Union address on January 28, 2008, President Bush did not specifically address ANWR. However, in a broader statement that was far less confrontational to Congress, he stated:

> The United States is committed to strengthening our energy security and confronting global climate change. And the best way to meet these goals is for America to continue leading the way toward the development of cleaner and more energy-efficient technology.

This last sentence was clearly aimed at promoting clean coal technology.

However, a White House news release entitled "Energy Security for the 21st Century" was posted subsequent to the State of the Union address. This document contained the following notation:

> As world demand for energy continues to increase, the president urges Congress to act on the remaining proposals from his energy security agenda....

We must increase our domestic supply of oil in a prudent and environmentally sensitive way. The president urges Congress to pass legislation that opens access to domestic energy sources in the outer continental shelf and Alaska and that protects America against supply disruptions by doubling the Strategic Petroleum Reserve.

Effectively, the eight-year run of the Bush administration came to a close with no resolution on ANWR. This was not surprising, given the contentious nature of the issues.

President Bush did achieve a major piece of energy legislation late in his second term, sans ANWR. In December 2007, the president signed the Energy Independence and Security Act of 2007. This act contained several significant provisions, namely the following:

- Increased the Corporate Average Fuel Economy (CAFÉ) standard to thirty-five miles per gallon by 2020

- Mandated reduced energy consumption in federal buildings by 30 percent by 2015

- Reduced annual petroleum consumption in federal government operations by 20 percent by 2015

- Increased use of alternative fuels in federal government operations by 10 percent by 2015

- Mandated increased production of biofuels to 36 billion gallons by 2022

- Mandated increased energy efficiency in light bulbs by 30 percent, phasing out most incandescent bulbs by 2012

- Mandated increased efficiency in selected appliances and encouraged the development of more efficient commercial buildings

Upon signing the Energy Independence and Security Act of 2007, President Bush again made reference to ANWR:

It's going to take time to transition to this new era. And we're still going to need hydrocarbons. And I hope the Congress will continue to open access to domestic energy sources—certain parts of the outer continental shelf and ANWR.

Congress would turn a deaf ear to the president's plea.

The 2008 presidential campaign and subsequent election of President Barack Obama and Vice President Joseph Biden ushered in a new era regarding energy policy in general and ANWR in particular.

The official Obama campaign Web site (www.barackobama.com), under the heading "Preserving Our Land," stated, "Barack Obama fought efforts to drill in the Arctic National Wildlife Refuge." In opposing legislation that would include drilling in ANWR, then-Senator Obama proclaimed:

> I strongly reject drilling in the Arctic National Wildlife Refuge because it would irreversibly damage a protected national wildlife refuge without creating sufficient oil supplies to meaningfully affect the global market price or have a discernible impact on U.S. energy security.

Interestingly, the official Obama White House Web site (www.whitehouse.gov) does not mention ANWR, despite an entire section devoted to energy and the environment. One could opine that, given a Democratic administration and a strong Democratic majority in Congress, drilling in ANWR is a dead issue. In addition, the ailing U.S. economy has captured the public's attention and will most likely hold center stage for some time to come. The staggering gas prices during the summer of 2008 have declined to more palatable levels and voters are no longer clamoring for relief from high energy prices.

Department of the Interior U.S. Fish and Wildlife Service (USFWS)

Dissension would also reign within the executive branch. The Department of the Interior U.S. Fish and Wildlife Service (USFWS), which currently manages ANWR, clearly indicated their preference in the environmental impact statement as far back as 1987–1988. Despite then Interior Secretary Hodel's recommendation to open the 1002 Area for leasing, the USFWS indicated their preference for no action. Page 221 of the environmental impact statement emphatically lays out their position:

> Alternative A [not to be confused with the alternative recommended by Hodel] is the Service's preferred alternative for managing the Arctic Refuge. This alternative, the "no action" alternative, would maintain the existing range and intensity of management and recreational and economic uses. It is assumed that existing laws, executive orders, regulations, and policies governing Service administration and operation of the National Wildlife Refuge System would remain in effect.

In essence, the USFWS expressed their desire to maintain ANWR as a minimal wildlife management area, in an undeveloped state, inclusive of the 1002 Area. As such, sport and subsistence hunting, trapping, and fishing would be allowed, and possibly even oil and gas studies (so long as they are considered to be compatible with refuge purposes). However, no leasing or hydrocarbon development would be permitted unless so directed by an act of Congress.

The underlying basis for the stance taken by the USFWS is that the Arctic Refuge contains several special traits that rate a Wilderness value designation. These traits are defined as wilderness, ecological, geological/paleontological, and scenic/recreational values. In the environmental impact statement, under chapter III on Special Values of the Arctic Refuge, the case for Wilderness designation was laid out:

> The Arctic Refuge's Wilderness qualities stand out among its many special values. The need to preserve a portion of the Brooks Range and arctic Alaska's great wilderness values formed the original basis for establishing the Arctic Range. Unlike many other refuges in the national wildlife refuge system, the Arctic Refuge was not established out of a singular need to conserve wildlife. Instead, the refuge was established out of a concern for the wilderness

ecosystem of northern Alaska as a whole—it was the physical features (tallest peaks in the Brooks Range, most glaciers, remoteness, and habitat diversity) and not the wildlife resources alone that originally drew focus to this area. Later field work reinforced the conviction that northeast Alaska was the best place to preserve an arctic wilderness ecosystem.

The above compelling argument made by the USFWS for designating ANWR as a Wilderness Area is one that has reverberated in Congress until this day.

Department of the Interior U.S. Geological Survey (USGS)

Second only to the U.S. Fish and Wildlife Service in terms of federal agency involvement in the future of ANWR, the U.S. Geological Survey (USGS) played a pivotal role in assessing the resource potential of ANWR and the 1002 Area in particular. Their petroleum assessment of 1998, which refined earlier resource estimates, concluded that the mean recoverable undiscovered oil for ANWR was 10.36 billion barrels. The 1002 Area accounted for 74 percent, or 7.7 billion barrels of technically recoverable oil. An economic analysis by the USGS indicated that, at $30 per barrel in 2003 dollars, approximately 73 to 82 percent of the technically recoverable oil would be deemed commercially viable, while at $55 per barrel, 90 percent would be considered economical.

The results of the petroleum assessment and economic analyses by the USGS provided the technical and commercial basis for advocating leasing in the 1002 Area. Without this information, the grounds for leasing would most likely be viewed as vague and conjectural. As such, the USGS were in a uniquely powerful role to influence the debate. However, much to their credit, they maintained a neutral position throughout, drawing a distinct line between policy and scientific investigation. Their mission was to conduct a petroleum assessment of ANWR, and that is what they did. Nowhere in the public record was this author able to extract a bias by the USGS in this matter.

In a USGS memo to the secretary of the interior dated April 5, 2002, the director of the USGS, Charles Groat, wrote the following:

Should the Congress approve petroleum development in the 1002 Area of the Arctic National Wildlife Refuge and given the commitment in the proposed legislation to minimizing the footprint and thereby the impacts on natural systems, there will be discussions about how to accomplish this and how to mitigate those impacts that occur. The model used in the work described in the referenced report [*Arctic Wildlife Coastal Plain Terrestrial Wildlife Summaries*] and complementary capabilities of our scientists are available to help you and other decision makers in the Department of the Interior assess proposed development plans and suggest ways to minimize and mitigate impacts. We stand ready to provide technical assistance to you and others involved in this important work.

The above statement from the USGS director essentially summarized the role of the USGS regarding ANWR: to be strictly that of providing technical assistance. To this end, they have performed true to mission.

U.S. Department of Energy (DOE)

Predictably, the U.S. Department of Energy (DOE) has played a significant role in the controversy surrounding ANWR. Within the DOE, however, there are both policy and non-policy entities. Prominent within these two spheres are the Office of Fossil Energy and the Energy Information Administration (EIA).

A Natural Gas Facts paper entitled "Arctic National Wildlife Refuge," published in June 2004 by the Office of Fossil Energy's National Energy Technology Laboratory, states the following:

ANWR is about the size of South Carolina, and the proposed development area in the coastal plain is about one-fifth the size of Washington, DC's Dulles International Airport.

ANWR could produce greater than a million barrels of oil per day (MMOPD), more than enough to replace U.S. imports from Iraq.

ANWR could produce more than 150 billion cubic feet of natural gas per year, which is about the volume of gas consumed by the state of South Carolina in 2000.

The Bush administration is in favor of opening ANWR for drilling, but there does not appear to be sufficient votes in the Senate to support the issue.

The state [Alaska] legislature passed a resolution supporting ANWR development by 60 votes to 0.

Oil and gas producers support drilling in ANWR and believe exploration can be done in an environmentally safe manner.

Annual polls show that over 75% [of Alaska citizens] support opening ANWR.

Environmental groups oppose drilling in ANWR because of its environmental and ecological value.

In a March 16, 2005, press release from the DOE Office of Public Affairs, Energy Secretary Samuel Bodman expressed his approval of a Senate budget resolution that included provisions for leasing in ANWR:

The Senate's vote today to clear the way for environmentally responsible oil and gas exploration in a small portion of ANWR is a victory for American consumers, America's economy, and America's energy security.

Alaska's frozen tundra has the potential to yield billions of barrels of domestically produced oil. Not only could these resources have a meaningful impact on our dependence on imported sources of oil: this means American jobs producing American oil for Americans.

The Senate action mentioned above did not yield tangible results. The role of the legislature will be covered in greater detail under the heading of "Legislative History."

In another DOE press release, from May 31, 2006, Secretary Bodman weighed in on the House bill entitled "American-Made Energy and Good Jobs Act":

I applaud the House's passage of a bill that allows

> responsible, environmentally safe oil and natural gas drilling in the ANWR region of arctic Alaska. Had President Clinton not vetoed the ANWR drilling bill in 1995, we would have at least an additional 1 million barrels a day of domestic oil production available to citizens of this country today.

While Secretary Bodman had an arguable point regarding the delays in passage of a bill that opens the 1002 Area to exploration and development, he gave the distinct impression that the reserves are already proven and merely waiting to be produced and delivered to market. At the same time, had ANWR been opened for leasing as far back as 1995, any commercially discovered reserves would most likely have already commenced production.

More recently, on February 26, 2008, Katherine Fredriksen, from the DOE Office of Policy and International Affairs, testified before the Senate Energy and Natural Resources Committee. The thrust of the testimony centered on increasing oil reserves for the Strategic Petroleum Reserve, but ANWR once again entered into the picture:

> In 2006, the United States imported over 12 million barrels of petroleum a day, accounting for roughly 60% of our daily consumption.
>
> We must confront the reasons we are dependent on foreign oil, and how we can mitigate these circumstances, including increased domestic exploration and production. Our domestic exploration has nearly bottomed out. Despite all the concern about reliance on foreign oil, this nation continues to forego available self-help: the tremendous resource available in ANWR and the vast majority of the outer continental shelf. The department is continually working to develop energy sources and improve our existing energy infrastructure and eliminate road blocks to that progress.

The relevant non-policy agency with the Department of Energy is the Energy Information Administration (EIA). This agency is the independent statistical and analytical arm of the DOE. It does not advocate a policy position on behalf of the DOE or the administration. As such, it is analytically neutral, which is somewhat of a rarity with respect to ANWR.

On February 23, 2004, the EIA was directed to address hydrocarbon production in ANWR by Richard Pombo, chairman of the U.S. House Committee on Resources. Specifically, the EIA was asked to assess the impact of oil and gas production in ANWR with respect to the EIA "Annual Energy Outlook 2004." In response to the chairman's request, the EIA produced the report, entitled "Analysis of Oil and Gas Production in the Arctic National Wildlife Refuge," in March 2004.

Critical to the EIA analysis is the time to first production. It was determined that seven to twelve years were required from the time of approval for leasing until first production. Reasons given for the five-year differential were delays caused by environmental considerations and drilling restrictions. Rather than make analytical determinations based on a range (seven to twelve years), it was assumed that first production would occur in 2013, approximately ten years after passage of enabling legislation. It was further assumed that the first lease sale would transpire twenty-two months after enactment of the bill. Given production start-up in 2013, ANWR would attain peak oil production of 0.9 million barrels per day by 2025. This production would come from several fields of varying reserve sizes, ranging from 1.4 billion barrels to 360 million barrels per field. The field sizes are based on the U.S. Geological Survey resource assessment for ANWR and represent the statistical mean for total reserves and individual field size. It should be noted that a high resource case for reserves puts peak oil production at 1.595 million barrels per day by 2023.

The EIA report concluded that oil development on the ANWR coastal plain would have the following impact:

- Reduced dependence on imported foreign oil in 2025 from 70 percent to 66 percent

- Improved U.S. balance of trade by $8 billion in 2025 (in 2002 dollars)

- Extended life of the Trans Alaskan Pipeline System

- Increased U.S. jobs (numbers not specified in the report)

- Reduced world oil prices (this would only occur if world supplies exceeded global demand)

Natural gas resources in ANWR were not projected to have an immediate impact, as it was presumed that the substantial gas reserves from the Prudhoe Bay complex and the National Petroleum Reserve—Alaska (NPR-A) were more than enough to satisfy the 51 trillion cubic feet needed to justify construction of an Alaskan gas pipeline.

The EIA report did highlight a few of the uncertainties inherent in their analysis of oil production in ANWR, namely the following:

The size of the resource base. The reserves are based on the best estimate of the range of oil and gas reserves, and are derived mainly from sparse seismic data, nearby wells, and analogs to the Prudhoe Bay Field complex. These are not proven reserves. Actual reserves could be larger or smaller.

The size of the fields. As above, the field sizes in the report are estimates only and are not actual. Larger field sizes could result in increased production, which would exceed the 0.9 million-barrel-per-day projection. Smaller field sizes would have the opposite effect.

The cost of developing the oil. These costs are often based on the quality of the oil, the character of the reservoir, and the distance to treatment and transportation facilities. In other words, they can be highly variable.

The timing of production. The report projected that production start-up would occur in 2013. This was based on the assumption that enabling legislation would pass in 2004. That did not happen. Instead, it may be prudent to project a production start-up will transpire anywhere from seven to twelve years from the award of leases.

Environmental considerations. These could affect timing of exploration and production, especially if legal challenges are made. They could also restrict access to resource potential areas and could also impact timing and location of pipelines, roads, and airstrips.

The 2004 EIA analysis would need to be updated if enabling legislation actually passed, to reflect the following:

- The current cost in both the price of oil and the cost to explore and develop

- Technological innovations in the energy industry

- The prevailing environmental concerns

Environmental Protection Agency (EPA)

Since its inception in 1970, the mission of the Environmental Protection Agency (EPA) has been to protect human health and the environment with respect to air, land, and water quality. The EPA is headed by an administrator who is appointed by the president. This position was elevated to cabinet rank during the George W. Bush administration. The EPA implements and enforces environmental regulations enacted by the U.S. Congress. The agency can delegate permitting and enforcement authority to state agencies and native tribes. If environmental standards and safeguards are not met, the EPA can also issue sanctions.

The EPA, while headquartered in Washington, DC, maintains ten regional offices throughout the country. Region 10, based in Seattle, encompasses the Pacific Northwest and Alaska, including tribal lands. The Region 10 published strategy for 2007–2011 has as one of its priorities:

> the appropriate application of EPA authorities related to oil and gas exploration, development, and production in Alaska to maximize permitting efficiencies and maintain environmental standards.
>
> EPA will exercise its authorities in a timely and coordinated manner in the oil and gas sector in Alaska to meet the highest standards of environmental and subsistence resource protection, while not unnecessarily limiting or restricting industry in contributing to the energy needs of the United States.

Hence, the EPA is one of the lead permitting agencies and, as a result, sits squarely in the crosshairs of competing entities with respect to ANWR. One can expect the permitting process for oil and gas activities in the 1002 Area to be protracted, complex, and costly. Permitting is also a major component in the Energy Information Administration's projection for production start-up in ANWR to run anywhere from seven to twelve years from date of license award.

Legislative Branch: History of Legislative Activity

Once the "Comprehensive Conservation Plan and Environmental Impact Statement" was published in 1987, the hurdle was cleared for congressional consideration of leasing in ANWR. The ensuing years led to considerable legislative activity and much heated debate but yielded no action in favor of leasing. While it is tempting to generalize by stating that Republicans are in favor of leasing and Democrats are opposed, there are exceptions. And this generalization cannot entirely explain the failure of the Republican-dominated Congress to pass leasing legislation during the first six years of the Bush administration. As of this writing, the Republicans are in the minority for the 111th Congress (2009–2010), and any attempt to introduce legislation to allow drilling in ANWR would surely fail. Quite the contrary, it would not be surprising to see legislation introduced that would declare all of ANWR to be a Wilderness Area, thereby permanently prohibiting drilling.

Given the many attempts to inject ANWR into Senate or House bills over the past two decades, unearthing this rich history would have been a monumental task were it not already provided by the Congressional Research Service. The Congressional Research Service provides research and policy analysis services to members of Congress. The service can take the form of reports, briefings, consultations, and congressional testimony. CRS research, when in report format, is readily available to the public. The CRS report for Congress dated September 2, 2008, entitled "Arctic National Wildlife Refuge (ANWR): Votes and Legislative Actions, 95th Congress to 110th Congress," lays out in table format the vote results taken by members of both the House and Senate regarding ANWR (see Table One and Table Two).

Table One: Votes in the House of Representatives on Energy Development within the Arctic National Wildlife Refuge (CRS Code: RL32838)

Congress	Date	Voice/ Roll Call	Brief Description
95th			no floor votes
96th	5/16/79	#152	Udall-Anderson substitute for H.R. 39 adopted by House (268-157); included provisions designating all of ANWR as Wilderness.
	5/16/79	#153	H.R. 39 passed House (360-65).

	11/12/80	voice (unanimous)	Senate version (leaving 1002 Area development issue to a future Congress) of H.R. 39 passed House.
97th			no floor votes
98th			no floor votes
99th			no floor votes
100th			no floor votes
101st			no floor votes
102nd			no floor votes
103rd			no floor votes
104th	11/17/95	#812	House agreed (237-189) to conference report on H.R. 2491 (H.Rept. 104-350), FY1996 budget reconciliation (a large bill that included 1002 Area development provisions; see text).
105th			no floor votes
106th			no floor votes
107th	8/1/01	#316	House passed Sununu amendment to H.R. 4 to limit specified surface development of 1002 Area to a total of 2,000 acres (228-201).
	8/1/01	#317	House rejected Markey-Johnson (CT) amendment to H.R. 4 to strike 1002 Area development title (206-223).
	8/2/01	#320	H.R. 4, an omnibus energy bill, passed House (240-189). Title V of Division F contained 1002 Area development provisions.
108th	4/10/03	#134	House passed Wilson (NM) amendment to H.R. 6 to limit certain features of 1002 Area development to a total of 2,000 acres (226-202).
	4/10/03	#135	House rejected Markey-Johnson (CT) amendment to H.R. 6 to strike 1002 Area development title (197-228).
	4/11/03	#145	House passed H.R. 6, a comprehensive energy bill (247-175); Division C, Title IV would have opened the 1002 Area to energy development.

Congress	Date	Voice/ Roll Call	Brief Description
109th	3/17/05	#88	House adopted (218-214) the concurrent budget resolution, H.Con.Res. 95, which included spending targets that would be difficult to achieve unless ANWR development legislation was passed.
	4/20/05	#122	House rejected (200-231) Markey amendment to strike the ANWR provision in its omnibus energy bill (H.R. 6) allowing leases for exploration, development, and production in ANWR.
	4/21/05	#132	House passed an omnibus energy bill (H.R. 6) with an ANWR development title (249-183).
	4/28/05	#149	House adopted (214-211) the conference report on the concurrent budget resolution, H.Con.Res. 95.
	12/18/05	#669	House adopted (308-106) the conference report on the defense appropriations bill (H.R. 2863), which would have allowed oil and gas leasing in ANWR.
	12/22/05	voice	House passed S.Con.Res. 74, which corrected the enrollment of H.R. 2863, removing the ANWR development provision.
	5/25/06	#209	House passed H.R. 5429 to open ANWR to development (225-201).
110th	8/4/07	#831	House rejected motion to recommit H.R. 3221 to the Energy and Commerce Committee with instructions to report back with language authorizing ANWR development (169-244).
	5/14/08	#321	House rejected motion to instruct conferees for S.Con.Res. 70 to adjust budget levels to assume increased revenues from opening ANWR to development (185-229).

Table Two: Votes in the Senate on Energy Development within the Arctic National Wildlife Refuge (CRS Code: RL32838)

Congress	Date	Voice/ Roll Call	Brief Description
95th			no floor votes
96th	7/22-23/80	#304	Motion to table Tsongas amendment (including a title to designate all of ANWR as Wilderness) to H.R. 39 defeated (33-64).
	8/18/80	#354	Senate adopted cloture motion on H.R. 39 (63-25).
	8/19/80	#359	Senate passed Tsongas-Roth-Jackson-Hatfield substitute to H.R. 39 (78-14); this bill is current law, and leaves decision about any 1002 Area development for a future Congress.
97th			no floor votes

Congress	Date	Voice/ Roll Call	Brief Description
98th			no floor votes
99th			no floor votes
100th			no floor votes
101st			no floor votes
102nd	11/1/91	#242	Cloture motion on S. 1220 failed; one title would have opened 1002 Area to development (50-44).
103rd			no floor votes
104th	5/24/95	#190	Senate voted to table Roth amendment to strip 1002 Area revenue assumptions from S.Con. Res. 13 (56-44).
	10/27/95	#525	Senate voted to table Baucus amendment to strip 1002 Area development provisions in H.R. 2491 (51-48).
105th			no floor votes
106th	4/6/00	#58	Senate voted to table Roth amendment to strip 1002 Area revenue assumptions from the FY2001 budget resolution (S.Con.Res. 101) (51-49).

107th	12/3/01	#344	Lott-Murkowski-Brownback amendment to Daschle amendment to H.R. 10 included 1002 Area development title in H.R. 4, as passed by the House. A cloture motion on the amendment failed (1-94).
	4/18/02	#71	Senate failed to invoke cloture on Murkowski amendment to S. 517, an omnibus energy bill. ANWR language of the amendment was similar to that in the House-passed version of H.R. 4 (46-54).
108th	3/19/03	#59	Senate passed Boxer amendment to delete certain revenue assumptions from S.Con.Res. 23, the FY2004 budget resolution; floor debate indicated that the amendment was clearly seen as a vote on developing the 1002 Area (52-48).
109th	3/16/05	#52	Senate voted to reject Cantwell amendment to strike revenue assumptions from its FY2006 budget resolution (S.Con.Res. 18) that would have given procedural protection to legislation authorizing oil drilling in part of ANWR (49-51).
	11/3/05	#288	Senate voted to reject Cantwell amendment to its FY2006 budget reconciliation bill (S. 1932) that would have deleted the provision establishing an oil and gas leasing program in ANWR (48-51).
	12/21/05	#364	Senate failed to invoke cloture on the conference report on the FY2006 Defense appropriations bill (H.R. 2863), which included provisions to open ANWR to development (56-44).

Congress	Date	Voice/ Roll Call	Brief Description
	12/21/05	#365	Senate adopted a concurrent resolution (S.Con.Res. 74) that instructed the Clerk of the House to strike provisions from the conference report to H.R. 2863 that would have allowed oil drilling in ANWR (48-45).

	3/16/06	#74	Senate passed the FY2007 budget resolution (S.Con.Res. 83) with a reconciliation instruction (§201) directing the Committee on Energy and Natural Resources to reduce budget authority by an amount equal to assumed revenues from development in ANWR (51-49).
110th	5/13/08	#123	Senate rejected (42-56) McConnell amendment (S.Amdt. 4720) to S. 2284 to open ANWR to energy development; earlier unanimous consent agreement had raised majority for adoption of amendment to 60 votes.

This particular report reaches as far back as the 96th Congress in 1979, when a failed attempt was made to designate all of ANWR as Wilderness Area. It concludes with the 110th Congress in 2008.

During the 108th Congress in 2003, the House proposed an energy bill that would have opened ANWR to energy development (H.R. 6). This provision was stricken from the Senate bill, and any reference to ANWR was deleted in conference. Noteworthy of this particular House bill was a provision to limit oil production facilities to 2,000 acres while exploration licenses would not be bound by such a restriction. Specifically, Section 30407(a)2 of H.R.6 states:

"ensure that the maximum amount of surface acreage covered by production and support facilities, including airstrips and any areas covered by gravel berms or piers for support of pipelines, does not exceed 2,000 acres on the coastal plain."

It was no doubt hoped that such a limitation would be more palatable to opponents of leasing and thus expedite passage of the bill. The attempt failed.

Subsequent to the above-referenced CRS report, additional updates were made available. During the first session of the 109th Congress, ANWR was added to the defense appropriations bill in the House (H.R. 2863) but failed in the Senate. In the second session of the 109th Congress, the Senate passed budget resolution FY2007 (S.Con. Res. 83), in March 2006, which included revenues from a lease sale in ANWR. Just two months later, on May 25, 2006, the House passed the American-Made Energy and Good Jobs Act (H.R. 5429). This act would also have allowed leasing and energy development in the 1002 Area of ANWR. Neither the Senate nor House bills were passed with the ANWR provision intact.

The Democrat-dominated first session of the 110th Congress lost little time in addressing ANWR. On January 4, 2007, Congressman Edward Markey (D-MA) introduced legislation (H.R.39) that would designate the coastal plain of ANWR, including the 1002 Area, as Wilderness, thus forever precluding energy development. This bill, also known as the Udall-Eisenhower Arctic Wilderness Act, was referred to the House Committee on Natural Resources, where it died a quiet death.

Congressional Activists

Congressional sentiment regarding ANWR runs strong in both houses. Opponents of leasing are championed by Senators Barbara Boxer (D-CA) and Joseph Lieberman (I-CT). In the House, Congressman Edward Markey (D-MA) leads the effort. Senator Boxer chairs the crucial Senate Committee on Environment and Public Works. Her Web site states that "she has led the fight to protect the California coast and the Arctic National Wildlife Refuge from oil drilling."

Senator Boxer is credited with having successfully led the battles on the House floor, in 2003 and again in 2005, to block bills that would have permitted leasing in ANWR.

Senator Joseph Lieberman (I-CT) is registered as an Independent but caucuses with the Democrats. He is also a member of the Senate Environment and Public Works Committee. On November 7, 2007, he introduced a bill to permanently designate all of ANWR as Wilderness Area, thus prohibiting oil and gas exploration. Senator Lieberman is credited with blocking legislation to allow leasing in ANWR in 1991, 1995, 2001, and 2003.

In the House of Representatives, Congressman Edward Markey (D-MA) chairs the powerful Select Committee on Energy Independence and Global Warming. He also sits on the Natural Resources Committee. In 2005, Congressman Markey led a successful effort to strip a provision to open ANWR for leasing from a budget bill. In an eloquent speech delivered on September 20, 2005, a day little known as Arctic Refuge

Action Day, Congressman Markey blasted the Bush administration and the Republicans in Congress for pursuing leasing in ANWR:

> President Roosevelt gave the country the New Deal—now President Bush wants to give the country a "raw deal."

> The reality is that Republican leaders are giving America a false choice. We do not have to choose between drilling in the Arctic Refuge or being at the mercy of oil from the Middle East. Drilling in the Refuge is completely unnecessary when we could improve the average fuel economy of cars, minivans, and SUVs by just three miles a gallon and save more oil within ten years than we could ever produce from the Arctic Refuge.

As previously stated, Congressman Markey advanced legislation in the 110th Congress to permanently designate ANWR as a Wilderness Area.

As one might expect, congressional advocates of leasing in the 1002 Area of ANWR have historically been led by the Alaskan delegation, namely Senators Ted Stevens and Lisa Murkowski, and Congressman Don Young. In response to Senator Lieberman's 2007 bill to designate all of ANWR as Wilderness Area, Stevens, Murkowski, and Young issued a joint proclamation on November 7, 2007:

> With the price of oil approaching $100 per barrel and with our energy independence on hostile foreign nations at a record high, now is not the time to cut our country off from the resources held in Alaska's coastal plain. The area has the largest untapped domestic oil field in the United States and would provide our nation with a million barrels of oil per day for at least three decades.

> We will fight any attempt to deny development of our state's resources, particularly the coastal plain. Alaska already contains vast lands designated as Wilderness,

including 8 million acres south of the coastal plain. Wilderness Areas in Alaska already exceed 58 million acres. More importantly, more than 192 million acres of Alaska are already protected in wilderness areas, national parks, national preserves, national forests, national wildlife refuges, wild and scenic rivers, state parks, state preserves, state critical habitat areas, and state marine parks. The total designated area is the equivalent of all the East Coast seaboard states from Maine to mid-Florida.

ANWR is nearly 20 million acres. Energy production would be limited to 2,000 acres—0.01 percent of the entire Refuge. In addition, development poses no threat to wildlife. Anti-development advocates claim that the Prudhoe Bay oil fields have had serious impacts on wildlife. That is not true. After thirty years of development of oil fields at Prudhoe Bay and surrounding areas, wildlife have not been adversely impacted. Populations of caribou, grizzly bears, polar bears, arctic foxes, and musk-ox have all remained stable or increased during oil exploration and development.

On March 13, 2008, Senator Lisa Murkowski proposed legislation that would open the 1002 Area of ANWR to leasing once the price of oil reached $125 per barrel. This bill, the American Energy Independence and Security Act of 2008, was co-sponsored by Senator Ted Stevens. Specifically, the legislation would automatically allow exploration and development of 1.5 million acres in ANWR once the world price of oil attained $125 per barrel for a minimum of five days. As in previous bills, production facilities would be limited to 2,000 acres. The bill also mandated (1) directional drilling so as to minimize the number of drill pads employed, (2) winter-only exploration, and (3) the use of ice roads that would disappear during the summer so as to minimize the impact on wildlife.

Royalties and tax revenues from ANWR development would be designated toward funding alternative energy programs, low-income home energy assistance, and the Women's, Infant's and Children's Nutrition Program.

No doubt it was hoped that the somewhat altruistic funding designation would help sway some opponents of leasing.

Congressman Young, the ranking Republican member of the House Resources Committee, announced his intention to draft similar supporting legislation in the House with the following comment:

> This delegation has tried repeatedly to open this minute portion of the 19 million acre Arctic Refuge. If Bill Clinton had not vetoed the budget bill containing ANWR in 1995, we might not be facing as severe an oil crisis today, and it is a shame that Congress has not opened ANWR before now. I fully support the actions Sens. Murkowski and Stevens are taking in the Senate; it is a commendable step in the right direction to making this country more energy independent. I am also in the process of drafting on a comprehensive energy bill in the House. This Congress has not produced a single piece of legislation that actually produces energy since the Trans Alaska Pipeline in 1973 and because we have not acted, Americans are struggling to pay their heating bills.

And so the battle rages on, with advocates and opponents alike releasing an endless barrage of hyperbole.

In the national elections of 2008, long-serving Alaska Republican Senator Ted Stevens was defeated by Anchorage Mayor Democrat Mark Begich. Although expected to vote with the Democrats on most initiatives, Senator Begich has made it clear that he favors drilling in ANWR and would oppose any legislation that prohibited drilling.

Chapter IX: The State of Alaska

The Permanent Fund and Revenue Distribution

Without a doubt, the economy of Alaska stands to benefit tremendously from development of the 1002 Area of ANWR, which explains why the Alaskan delegation to Congress is among the most ardent proponents of leasing.

Should a bill similar to H.R. 6, the Arctic Coastal Plain Domestic Energy Security Act of 2003, be passed by Congress, 50 percent of the bonus bids and rental and royalty payments would go to the state of Alaska. In addition, this bill would direct the U.S. Treasury Department to establish a Coastal Plain Local Government Impact Aid Assistance Fund from a portion of the federal revenues. This fund would provide federal assistance to "the North Slope Borough, Kaktovik and other boroughs, municipal subdivisions, villages and any other community organized under Alaska State law." To the layperson, this would include every single community in Alaska.

It is estimated that oil revenues have accounted for approximately 80 percent of total state revenues over several decades. According to a 2004 University of Alaska report by Terence Cole and Pamela Cravez entitled "Blinded by Riches: The Prudhoe Bay Effect", more than 80 percent of the $350 billion in resource generation from 1959 to 2002 came from the North Slope oil fields.

Although estimates vary greatly as to the extent of the financial impact on the Alaskan economy of a commercial discovery in ANWR, certainly billions of dollars over several decades would be generated. While some communities would benefit more than others, every resident in Alaska receives an annual dividend from the State of Alaska

Permanent Fund that is generated from oil and gas revenues. In 2007, the distribution from this fund resulted in a dividend payment of $1,654 to all 604,149 residents of Alaska.

The Alaska Permanent Fund was established by a state constitutional amendment in 1976. The amendment and resulting statutes set aside at least 25 percent of mineral revenues into dedicated accounts that are invested for the benefit of current and future generations of Alaskans. The very first deposit into the Permanent Fund of $734,000, primarily from lease bonuses, took place on February 28, 1977. As of April 2008, the fund contained a little over $38 billion in assets, most of which were invested in stocks, bonds, CDs, and real estate. The Permanent Fund is managed by the Alaska Permanent Fund Corporation (APFC), a quasi-independent state entity directed by a six-member board of trustees. The state legislature provides audit and accountability oversight, with the APFC annual budget requiring legislative approval. The annual dividends are distributed by the Permanent Fund Dividend Division of the Alaskan Department of Revenue.

The annual dividend is calculated according to a set formula, which takes into account the fund's net income over the last five years, the operating cost of the program, and the statutory percentage allocated for dividend distribution. The largest dividend amount was $1,963.86 in 2000, with the smallest dividend being $331.29 in 1984. With the creation of the Permanent Fund, Alaska has managed to create and maintain a permanent source of revenue from a resource that is nonrenewable and easily depleted. In fiscal year 2007, the fund earned $3.428 billion in statutory net income, thus assuring Alaskans of a dividend check for many years to come.

Alaskan Sentiment

Alaskan sentiment regarding leasing in ANWR runs strong, in both directions. Historically, the majority of Alaskans support drilling in the 1002 Area of ANWR. According to a poll conducted by Dittman Research Corporation of Alaska in 2000, 75 percent of respondents indicated that oil and gas exploration should be allowed within the coastal plain of ANWR, while 23 percent felt exploration should not be allowed. Of the 23 percent who responded negatively to exploration, 36 percent indicated they would reverse their position if three-dimensional seismic techniques were employed, which would presumably reduce the environmental impact of exploration. This is somewhat consistent with polls that have taken place throughout the controversial life of ANWR, with an average 69 percent of Alaskans favoring exploration, while 25 percent were opposed and 6 percent were undecided. Nationwide public opinion polls regarding ANWR reflect a somewhat mixed sentiment and will be covered in more detail in a later chapter.

The government of Alaska, administrations both past and present, has steadfastly supported leasing in ANWR. The former governor, Sarah Palin, made it clear that her administration would follow the same course. When U.S. Senator Joe Lieberman initiated a bill to permanently designate the entire ANWR as Wilderness Area, Governor Palin sent a strongly worded letter to the senator on November 9, 2007, stating:

> With the price of oil hovering around $100 per barrel, I was astonished to learn that you, with 25 co-sponsors, have introduced legislation that would permanently block the development of oil and natural gas in the most promising unexplored petroleum province in North America—the coastal plain of the Arctic National Wildlife Refuge (ANWR) in Alaska.
>
> The development of ANWR would reduce U.S. dependence on unstable sources of crude oil, such as the Middle East, and would decrease the U.S. trade deficit, a large percentage of which is directly attributable to importing crude oil, now totaling more than 60% of daily consumption.
>
> If ANWR had been developed as proposed in the 1980s or 1990s, the U.S. would now be enjoying the benefits of this resource. So, the argument advanced by drilling opponents that ANWR oil would not help the nation for several years—the time required to develop a small portion of the coastal plain—is disingenuous ands simply serves to delay a critical policy decision.

As the Republican vice presidential candidate in the 2008 election, Governor Palin maintained her unwavering stance in favor of leasing in ANWR. She lost no opportunity to promote ANWR development in the context of energy security and job growth. However, her running mate, Senator John McCain, purposely ignored ANWR while simultaneously campaigning in favor of increased domestic energy exploration. Although this omission by McCain may have been intended to mute criticism by environmental organizations, it did him little good when the election results were finally tallied.

Alaskan Job Growth

Efforts to assess the economic impact of developing ANWR on the Alaskan and national economy have taken on near mythic proportions. In 2003, the National Defense Council Foundation (NDCF) in Alexandria, Virginia, published its findings on ANWR job and revenue creation. Entitled "The Economic Impact of Developing ANWR Resources," it projected direct nationwide job creation from ANWR to be 628,144 and indirect job growth to be 446,496, for a total of 1,074,640 over the life of ANWR development.

Many of the direct jobs would include manufacturing in addition to personnel directly employed in the petroleum industry. Indirect jobs would employ the multiplier effect, thereby encompassing such sectors as services, transportation, and government.

Alaska would see substantial job creation, with 94,733 direct and 67,333 indirect jobs created, for a total 162,066. Currently, approximately 2,500 Alaskans are directly employed in the oil and gas sector (*Alaska Economic Trends*, November 2006). This number is projected to essentially remain static if ANWR is not developed. Hence, ANWR job creation would represent an exponential boon to Alaskans, in new jobs, in the state coffers and local economies, and in substantial additions to the Permanent Fund.

It should be noted that the above job growth numbers have been cited extensively by leasing proponents, particularly by members of Congress as well as the Teamsters Union. At the same time, leasing opponents have challenged the veracity of those statistics. It stands to reason that the majority of jobs created would be short-lived, as fields are discovered and developed, and production facilities are built. Once the infrastructure is in place, however, one would expect the numbers to decline significantly, and possibly approach the same order of magnitude as the current employment numbers for the North Slope fields.

Native Alaskans
The Arctic Slope Regional Corporation

The Arctic Slope Regional Corporation (ASRC) is a private corporation, owned and operated by native Alaskans, for the benefit of the Inupiat Alaskans. It is a for-profit entity and represents the business interests of eight villages on the Arctic Slope, including the city of Kaktovik, which is located within ANWR. Under the Alaskan Native Claims Settlement Act of 1971, ASRC was granted title to both surface and mineral rights to 5 million acres on the North Slope of Alaska.

ASRC has 9,000 shareholders and employs 6,000 people. Its founding principle is "to preserve the Inupiat culture and traditions." The ASRC companies include engineering and consulting services, civil construction, oil and gas support services, petroleum refining and distribution, aerospace engineering services, communications, venture capital management, and facilities management. These services are provided to both multinational corporations and government agencies.

ASRC also provides mineral leases to energy companies for exploration and development. The most successful ASRC mineral leasing area is in the Colville River Delta, located approximately fifty miles west of Prudhoe Bay. This area is the site of the giant Alpine Oil Field, which together with smaller satellite fields, contains roughly 500 million barrels of recoverable oil. About half the field is situated on ASRC lands, and the remainder is located on state leases. Alpine Field is the fifth-largest field on the North Slope and is currently operated by ConocoPhillips Alaska.

The goals established by ASRC in selecting the 5 million acres under its jurisdiction were clear:
"To gain title to the lands with the greatest resource potential,
"To explore and develop ASRC lands,
"To produce and market the resource from them."

To this end, ASRC has obtained the subsurface rights, which include mineral leasing, to 92,000 acres that surround the village of Kaktovik. The surface rights belong to the Kaktovik Inupiat Corporation (KIC).

ASRC, by its very charter and subsequent actions, is clearly a proponent of leasing in ANWR. The only well ever drilled in ANWR was the Chevron KIC#1, which was drilled in the 1980s on a lease from ASRC. The results of that well remain confidential to this day, known in the industry as a "tight hole."

Kaktovik

The Inupiat village of Kaktovik is located on Barter Island on the coastal plain of ANWR. It is the only native Alaskan settlement within the boundaries of ANWR. Barter Island began as a trade settlement for the Inupiat. Kaktovik was officially incorporated as a city on March 26, 1971, although the Inupiats look upon the village more as a base than a city. The 2000 census listed a population of 293 for Kaktovik, while ASRC indicates that there were 306 residents in 2001. A majority of the residents are Inupiat Eskimos.

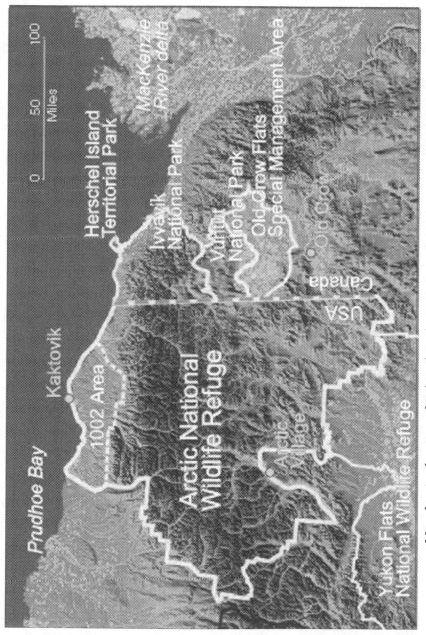

Map showing location of Kaktovik in the 1002 Area of ANWR: courtesy of USFWS

Over 40 percent of the citizens are employed by the North Slope Borough, and a quarter work for the school district. The remainder are employed in the private sector. Subsistence hunting and fishing, including whaling, are a significant element of the Inupiat culture. Native Alaskan arts and crafts are also produced and sold. Like most North Slope communities, Kaktovik is dry. Alcohol cannot be sold or possessed. Suicide among young native Alaskans runs three to four times higher than average, and alcohol appears to be a contributing factor.

For a small city, Kaktovik maintains an informative Web site (www. kaktovik.com), which highlights their rich cultural heritage and their strong ties to the land. It also addresses the great debate swirling about their lands, to wit:

> Do the Kaktovik support oil development or do they oppose it? Here the questions are not so simple and the issue is not so easily defined as to which side of this debate we support. That argument is not conceived here. The polemic surrounding ANWR was not created in Kaktovik, but constructed in the minds of two warring factions conspiring against one another in a place very far from here. It was created outside our place, so is of little consequence to us.
>
> We have carefully studied and taken a position on petroleum development. We have reached a consensus that we have held now for over two decades. The consensus is not what most people think, it is much more complex. The essence of the Kaktovik position is that we would support oil exploration and development of the coastal plain *provided* we are given the authority and resources to ensure that it is done properly and safely. Without the necessary provisions to ensure this protection, we would not.

The Kaktovik produced a rather thought-provoking document entitled *In This Place*, which was the result of the Kaktovik Impact Project and illustrated the concerns raised by the residents over petroleum development as well as intrusions from tourists and state and federal authorities. Much of the angst in this document is directed against helicopter traffic that disturbs the wildlife and the U.S. Fish and Wildlife Service, which oversees ANWR. Few outside interventions escape criticism, much of which is based on the view that little respect is given to the people of Kaktovik, their land, and their way of life. The oil companies do not escape these criticisms, but are afforded some respect, as follows:

> Finally, we must speak about the lines that have come onto your maps of our country by those who search for oil and gas. We know these people pretty well. We have worked with them in these matters. Unlike those others who have come to take our land, to make it theirs, to control it as they want it controlled, to drive us out, these people only want the oil, and, after we have had a few words with them about it, they have tried to work with us, to respect our interest in the country.

> They are rough, some of these oil people, but so are we, and we think we can deal with them. We and they both know and understand that someday they will be gone. They have no interest in staying here, in getting and holding our lands and waters. The lines they draw on the maps are not territorial lines, but temporary ones, and we feel we can live with them.

> If, as others say, they are devils, these oil people, then maybe they are the very ones with whom we have to deal. One thing we know for sure, if any deal with them, it should be us. It will be us. We trust no one else to do it for us.

Perhaps their most scathing indictment is reserved for the media:

> We see television crews who arrive without notice, with their script and stories written, what their message will be, already known and always wrong, into which they try to fit us, mixing our words and making us say

what we do not mean, as if by magic, as if they were witches.

So what exactly is the position of the Inupiats of Kaktovik regarding petroleum development in ANWR? Their impact statement emphasizes that they cannot be for or against something that has yet to be clearly defined as to its impact on their way of life. They desire a real voice in the process. Not a passive voice, but one that can exert both direct influence in a general sense and real authority where their way of life is concerned. The impact statement lays out a five-point plan that is designed to allow for oil development while simultaneously addressing the needs and concerns of their people. Among other provisions, the plan calls for a Kaktovik Impact Office and a central authority to handle all of the planning, permitting, and monitoring of industrial activity. Assuming such an authority and impact office was established, and the other elements of the proposed plan were met, then it is presumed that exploration and development activities could proceed with the blessings of, and in cooperation with, the native Alaskans of Kaktovik.

The Gwich'in

To the south of ANWR, on the banks of the east fork of the Chandalar River in the Brooks Range, lies Arctic Village. The village is situated approximately 125 miles south of the 1002 Area of ANWR.

The native Alaskan population of Arctic Village is 172 residents and is comprised mainly of Neets'ali Gwich'in. Their economy is for the most part subsistence based, although some seasonal employment does occur. The Gwich'in hunt Porcupine caribou, moose, sheep, rabbit, and waterfowl. They also rely on freshwater fish. The village is accessible via a gravel airstrip, but is otherwise quite remote.

Arctic Village is not a part of the Arctic Slope Regional Corporation and is too far south to be included in the North Slope Borough. Yet its voice regarding ANWR development is being heard and is in stark contrast to the position taken by the Inupiats of Kaktovik. The Gwitch'in are opposed to drilling in ANWR because they fear it will diminish the Porcupine caribou herd, which they rely upon for subsistence. The caribou migrate through and inhabit portions of ANWR during calving and post-calving periods. The Porcupine caribou range far, including the Brooks Range and in the vicinity of Arctic Village. The Gwich'in claim a cultural affinity for the caribou.

Approximately 7,000 Gwich'in inhabit fifteen villages in northwestern Canada and northeastern Alaska. In 1988, the Gwich'in from Arctic Village allied themselves with Gwich'in from neighboring Canada and formed the Gwich'in Steering Committee. The primary purpose of the steering committee was to oppose drilling in the 1002 Area of ANWR. The committee asserts that:

"drilling in the Arctic Refuge would violate the human rights of the Gwich'in people because of the impacts drilling would have on Gwich'in subsistence, culture, and way of life."

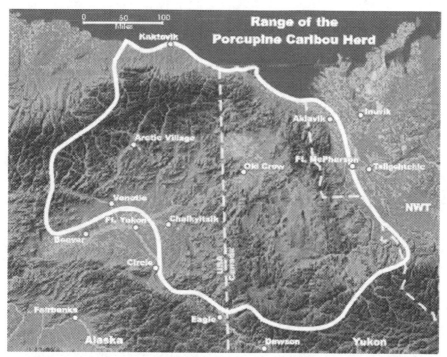

Map showing locations of Kaktovik and Arctic Village and range of the Porcupine caribou herd: courtesy of USFWS

In 2005, the Gwich'in Steering Committee published a report entitled "A Moral Choice for the United States." The report was prepared for the Gwich'in by the Episcopal Church, the director of the Human Rights Law Clinic at American University, and the public interest law firm known as the Trustees for Alaska.

The essence of the report is as follows:

The U.S. Congress is again considering opening the coastal plain of the Arctic National Wildlife Refuge to oil and gas drilling. The proposal threatens to violate the internationally recognized human rights to culture, subsistence, health and religion of the Gwich'in people of northeastern Alaska and northwestern Canada.

For thousands of years, the Gwich'in have relied on the caribou as their primary food source, and despite the inroads of modern civilization, that remains true today.

The Coastal Plain, and in particular the so-called "1002 Area" that is the focus of the oil exploration and development proposal, is vital calving and post-calving habitat for the Porcupine Caribou Herd.

Research has shown that oil drilling activity in critical caribou calving habitat, such as the coastal plain, displaces female caribou and calves, diminishing calf survival rates.

Because of the impact of drilling on the Porcupine Caribou Herd, opening the coastal plain of the Arctic National Wildlife Refuge would deal a serious blow to the ability of the Gwich'in to continue their subsistence culture that is reliant on the Porcupine Caribou Herd. Loss of this culture would violate the internationally recognized human rights of the Gwich'in to their own means of subsistence, to culture, to health, and to religion.

To this end, the Gwich'in staged a month-long protest during the summer of 2005 in Washington, DC, against a congressional bill to open the 1002 Area for leasing. The bill was subsequently defeated by a Democratic-led filibuster in the Senate. The Gwich'in rejoiced. The Inupiats of Kaktovik did not. The Kaktovik Impact Project, previously discussed, addresses their feelings for the Gwich'in of Arctic Village in somewhat couched language:

South of us we also hear occasional strange noises. We

were not aware of the dependency of the Gwitchin [sic] on our caribou. Indeed, we thought the caribou were unreliable in those parts, rather spooky and unpredictable, not nearly as sure as they are to be here to calve. We were under the impression that the Gwitchin [sic] had to depend on other things, especially fish, as we depend more on the sea than the land.

It is of interest to note that the Inupiats of Kaktovik refer to the caribou as "our caribou."

An Alaskan-based nongovernmental organization known as Arctic Power (more on this group in a later chapter) has also taken exception to the Gwich'in position regarding ANWR. The Arctic Power Web site, ANWR.org, paints an entirely different picture of the Gwich'in and their relationship to the Porcupine caribou. Arctic Power emphatically states the following:

The Gwich'in Indians

Are <u>NOT</u> indigenous to the coastal plain—some live south of ANWR, while the majority live in Canada,

Actively sought oil production on their own lands three times— unsuccessfully,

Leased their entire lands to Rougeot Oil and Gas Corp. in 1980 with lax provisions for their now "sacred" caribou.

National environmental organizations now provide the sustenance the Gwich'in couldn't get from oil.

The Porcupine Caribou Herd

ANWR opponents claim development will devastate the 123,000-member herd and its calving grounds.

Since 1983, not once has high-density calving taken place in the 1002 Area.

Greatest threat to the herd is their harsh natural habitat—a series of severe winters in the '90s depleted 15 percent of the herd.

Second greatest existing threat to the herd is the Gwich'in Indians of Canada—Gwich'in hunters kill 3,000 Porcupine caribou each year.

Alaskan Federation of Natives

The Alaskan Federation of Natives (AFN), based in Anchorage, is probably the most inclusive entity representing the native Alaskans. Founded in 1966, the AFN boasts a membership that encompasses 178 villages, 13 regional native corporations, and 12 regional nonprofit institutions and tribal consortiums. The Arctic Slope Regional Corporation is a member.

The AFN position regarding ANWR is clear and is published on their Web site (www.nativefederation.org) as a 2006 federal priority:

> AFN supports responsible and environmentally sound oil and gas development in the Arctic National Wildlife Refuge (ANWR). Responsible development will bring considerable economic benefits to Alaska, some of which should be devoted to promoting the economic and social welfare of Alaska natives.

The AFN also weighed in on the congressional bills relating to ANWR, as is evidenced by a letter dated April 19, 2005, encouraging support for exploration and reminding Congress that the village of Kaktovik is prevented from leasing on their 92,000 acres until the 1002 Area issue is resolved.

Hence, with the exception of the 172 Gwich'in of Arctic Village and their Canadian counterparts, the majority of native Alaskans have demonstrated in favor of opening the 1002 Area for leasing. This should not be construed as a blank check, however, as the native Alaskans, particularly the residents of Kaktovik, want to exercise some control over the process, and they especially want to share the economic benefits of any discovery.

Chapter X: Canada

THE GOVERNMENT OF CANADA has made its position on ANWR well known through its embassy in Washington, the environment minister, and the native Gwich'in of the Canadian Yukon. Canada is opposed to opening the 1002 Area for exploration and development. In 2001, the following statement was released by the Canadian Embassy, entitled "A Unique Ecosystem at Risk":

> Canada supports responsible development in habitats which are not critical. The calving grounds on the coastal plain of the Arctic Refuge are critical to the survival of the Porcupine caribou herd and to the culture and way of life of the Gwitchin [sic] people.
>
> Canada has protected its portion of the calving grounds. We urge the U.S. Congress and administration to do the same—to provide Wilderness protection to the calving grounds of the Porcupine caribou herd on the coastal plain of the Arctic National Wildlife Refuge.

In a July 17, 2001, letter to members of the U.S. House of Representatives, Canadian Ambassador Michael Kergin wrote, "Canada's view on drilling in the Arctic National Wildlife Refuge coastal plain is simple: Both countries are obligated to provide the same level of permanent protection for the Porcupine caribou herd."

While an exact count of the Porcupine caribou herd is difficult to determine, the Canadian Embassy lists their numbers at 129,000 and indicates their range extends from northeastern Alaska to the northern Yukon and the Mackenzie Delta in the Northwest Territories.

Migrations occur over 400 miles. The embassy confirms a Gwich'in population of 7,000 but does not indicate how many Porcupine caribou are harvested annually.

On July 17, 1987, the United States and Canada executed a non-binding agreement regarding the conservation of the Porcupine caribou herd. The objectives of the agreement were the following:

> To conserve the Porcupine caribou herd and its habitat through international cooperation and coordination so that the risk of irreversible damage or long-term adverse effects as a result of use of caribou or their habitat is minimized;
>
> To ensure opportunities for customary and traditional uses of the Porcupine caribou herd by rural Alaska residents and natives in the Yukon and Northwest Territories;
>
> To enable users of Porcupine caribou to participate in the international co-ordination of the conservation of the Porcupine caribou herd and its habitat;
>
> To encourage co-operation and communication among governments, users of Porcupine caribou, and others to achieve these objectives.

To this end, an International Porcupine Caribou Board was established to share information, conduct studies, and provide advice and recommendations in matters affecting the Porcupine caribou. While non-binding, this agreement between Canada and the United States is often cited when discussing the fate of ANWR.

The Inupiats of Kaktovik have taken particular exception to the Canadian perspective regarding ANWR. In their Kaktovik Impact Project paper, they address Canada's position:

> We would also like to comment to a certain degree of hypocrisy we witness from time to time. The Dempster Highway in the Yukon is surely the greatest single threat to the future well- being of the Porcupine caribou. It was built a few years ago without any hearings or thought with respect to that impact. We would be comforted

if the Canadian Wildlife Service and the Yukon Game
Branch were a bit more assertive in matters on their
side of things and a bit more respectful of us.

As an alternative to drilling in ANWR, in 2001 the Canadian
government attempted to entice the Bush administration to promote
U.S. investment in the oil sands in Alberta Province. Prime Minister
Jean Chretien advised President Bush that the potential oil reserves of
the Alberta oil sands exceeded those of Saudi Arabia. While this may be
true, extracting those reserves presents some unique and costly technical
challenges for the oil companies. And not every entity involved would
necessarily view ANWR and Alberta as mutually exclusive pursuits.

Chapter XI:
Wildlife, Environmental,
and Conservation Organizations

THERE ARE A PLETHORA of wildlife and environmental non-profit institutions that have registered their opposition to drilling in ANWR. This book lists eleven of the most prominent organizations. While there are certainly others immersed in the debate, it is proffered that those discussed herein essentially encompass the issues and concerns of the many. In researching these institutions, it became clear that their reasons and approaches to ANWR are profoundly varied. Those parties who favor exploration leasing in the 1002 Area of ANWR have sometimes compressed the opposition into a single entity and responded to them as such. They do so at their peril.

The following non-profit institutions are discussed, in alphabetical order:

- Alaska Coalition
- Alaska Wilderness League
- Center for Biological Diversity
- Environmental Defense Fund
- Green Century Capital Management
- Greenpeace
- Nature Conservancy
- Natural Resources Defense Council
- Sierra Club
- U.S. PIRG Arctic Wilderness Campaign
- World Wildlife Fund

Alaska Coalition

The Alaska Coalition represents a broad network of conservation, sporting, religious, and labor groups throughout the United States. It lists nearly 1,000 groups as belonging to the coalition. It is based in Alaska, and its entire focus is on protecting Alaskan wilderness areas.

The Alaska Coalition lists as a primary goal: "Prevent all attempts to open the Arctic National Wildlife Refuge to oil and gas drilling."

Toward this end, the coalition Web site (www.alaskacoalition.org) addresses most of the issues regarding ANWR:

1   Preserving wildlife, especially the polar bear, Porcupine caribou, and migratory birds

2   Respecting the culture and traditions of the Gwich'in

3   Not enough oil in ANWR to make a difference, nor reduce dependence on foreign oil

Its approach toward achieving its mission is straightforward:

1   Call your congressman

2   Conduct a grassroots campaign with friends and relatives

3   Write letters to the editors of local papers

4   Support H.R. 39, which would designate the entire Refuge as a Wilderness Area

An excerpt from the Alaska Coalition reads as follows:
Action Alert!

Help Permanently Protect the Arctic Refuge

On January 4, 2007, Representatives Ed Markey (D-MA) and Jim Ramstad (R-MN) introduced H.R. 39, a bill that would permanently protect the coastal plain of the Arctic National Wildlife Refuge. While this bill has been introduced in previous congressional sessions, the pro-conservation 110th Congress represents the best opportunity in years to build momentum towards passage of an Arctic Wilderness bill.

Interestingly, the Alaska Coalition Web site (www.alaskacoalition.org) suggests contacting the Alaska Wilderness League for more information and for ways to help and presumably contribute to the coalition. The Web site also contains maps that depict the federal public lands in Alaska. An astounding 200+ million acres of federal public lands are in Alaska, including fifteen national parks, sixteen national wildlife refuges, and two of our largest national forests.

The following statistics are derived from the Alaska Coalition Web site:

Current Land Statistics in Alaska

National Public Land Ownership

National Park Lands:

- **52.9 million acres (68% of nation's total acreage)**

- **33.5 million** acres in wilderness

    National Wildlife Refuge Lands

- **72.4 million** acres (**83%** of nation's total acreage)

- **18.7 million** acres in wilderness

    National Forest Service Lands

- **22.5 million** acres

- (The nation's two largest National Forests—Tongass more than **3** times larger than any other)

- **5.8 million** acres in wilderness

    BLM Lands: Approximately 70 million acres

- Alaska contains **365,500,000** acres of land

- Reference point: California is approximately **100 million** acres

Alaska Wilderness League

The Alaska Wilderness League is a 501(C)(3) non-profit corporation based in Washington, DC, whose sole mission is to protect the wilderness lands of Alaska, which includes ANWR. The league is a supporting member of the Alaska Coalition, discussed previously. Similar to the Alaska Coalition, the league employs a broad swath of issues to push for designating all of ANWR as Wilderness. Both native Alaskans and wildlife preservation (polar bears, Porcupine caribou, migratory birds) are discussed. However, the Inupiats of Kaktovik are mentioned on the league's Web site and included with the Gwich'in, as if to indicate the Inupiats are opposed to leasing in ANWR. This appears to be in direct contradiction to what the Inupiats of Kaktovik have stated in their Impact Report.

The major difference between the Alaska Wilderness League and the Alaska Coalition is the league has the federal government as its sole target audience, while the Alaska Coalition takes a wider approach, ranging from the U.S. Congress to local media and grassroots campaigning.

The league opened an Arctic Environmental Justice Center in Anchorage in January 2007. The center is intended to serve as a base of local support for their mission.

Center for Biological Diversity

The Center for Biological Diversity is a non-profit corporation based in Tucson, Arizona, that boasts 40,000 members. Its mission statement reads as follows:

> At the Center for Biological Diversity, we believe that the welfare of human beings is deeply linked to nature—to the existence in our world of a vast diversity of wild animals and plants. Because diversity has intrinsic value, and because its loss impoverishes society, we work to secure a future for all species, great and small, hovering on the brink of extinction. We do so through science, law, and creative media, with a focus on protecting the lands, waters, and climate that species need to survive.

> We want those that come after us to inherit a world
> where the wild is still alive.

The approach taken by the center to achieve its mission is highly focused and somewhat unique. The center draws upon the citizen petition provision in the Endangered Species Act to take legal recourse, either with the decision-making agency or through the courts, whether it be at the federal, state, or local level.

Regarding ANWR, the center's objective has been to protect the threatened or endangered species and their habitats from oil development. This now includes the polar bears and the bowhead whales. Thus, even if the 1002 Area were opened for leasing, a much higher standard of protection is now afforded the polar bears and their habitat, and one can expect the Center for Biological Diversity to be at the forefront of ensuring that standard is met.

Environmental Defense Fund

The Environmental Defense Fund (EDF) boasts a membership of more than 500,000. It is a New York-based activist organization with a focus on finding practical solutions to environmental problems. Regarding the Arctic National Wildlife Refuge, the activism occurs primarily at the federal level and entails petitioning Congress and the administration to oppose drilling in ANWR. Its Web site (www.edf. org) cites a number of facts that are somewhat dated and inaccurate with respect to ANWR. This element will be covered in greater detail in chapter XIV, Rhetoric vs. Reality.

The Environmental Defense Fund produces a publication entitled "Safe and Secure: Meeting America's Energy Needs" which offers potentially viable solutions to the energy crisis. The document frames these solutions in terms of U.S. economic and energy security as well as under the broader context of global climate change. It highlights renewable energy sources, energy efficiency, cogeneration, and distributed energy as solutions. Regarding distributed energy, EDF proposes building small power-generating stations closer to the end users. This approach is touted as being more energy efficient while also presenting less of a terrorist target due to its small size. All of the above recommendations are directly made to Congress.

The EDF incorporates economics along with science and law to advance its position. Its stated intent is to "evaluate environmental problems and work to create and advocate solutions that win lasting political, economic, and social support because they are nonpartisan, cost efficient, and fair."

What differentiates EDF from some other environmental organizations is its inclusion of economics, along with science and law, to bolster its position.

Green Century Capital Management

Green Century Capital Management (GCCM) presents a truly unique approach to environmental activism: shareholder advocacy. GCCM was founded by, and is wholly owned by, environmental non-profit organizations. Many of these institutions are state-based Public Interest Research Groups (PIRGs). Through its mutual funds, Green Century invests in companies in order to influence them to adopt stronger environmental policies. All of the profits earned by Green Century from the fund management fees are directed to the non-profit owners and used for advocacy purposes. Through the process of shareholder resolutions, Green Century's focus is to effect change in six major areas:

- Wilderness preservation and biodiversity

- Toxics and environmental health

- Pure water and safe food

- Clean air and energy

- Chemical security

- Political influence

Green Century has pursued shareholder advocacy actions regarding ANWR under the topic of wilderness preservation and biodiversity. Since its funds hold shares in ExxonMobil, ChevronTexaco, and ConocoPhillips, all of which are active on Alaska's North Slope, Green Century has engaged these companies through shareholder resolutions by requesting formal corporate policies on drilling in sensitive areas and withdrawal from the Arctic National Wildlife Refuge. While unable to obtain a majority of votes on the above resolutions, Green Century has gained influence in a relatively short time and has been credited with raising the environmental consciousness of independent shareholders as well.

Greenpeace

No other environmental organization captures media attention like Greenpeace. Known for its bold and aggressive activist polices, the group cut its teeth in 1971 by interfering with nuclear testing off the coast of Alaska with a small boat. Small boats inserted into the fray have become its best-known method of operations. Unlike most of the U.S.-based environmental non-profits previously discussed, Greenpeace is an international organization with offices in more than thirty countries. In the United States, the main office is located in Washington, DC. Membership is 2.5 million worldwide, with 250,000 in the United States alone.

Greenpeace has been at the forefront of environmental activism, having demonstrated against or interfered with commercial whaling operations and nuclear weapons testing throughout the globe. Rather than lobbying Congress to take action, Greenpeace takes direct action itself, an element that distinguishes it from most other environmental groups. In Alaska, the group has vigorously protested offshore drilling over concern for whales, only to have the U.S. Coast Guard drive protestors away from the area of operations.

Concerning ANWR, Greenpeace has taken a vocal stance, referring to ANWR as "America's Serengeti," a phrase echoed throughout by environmental groups. Greenpeace claims that Arctic wildlife has already been harmed by global warming and that the wildlife within the Refuge would be exposed to oil spills and pollution. The Washington, DC, office of Greenpeace advocates use of tax monies to fund renewable energy projects such as wind and solar energy.

The Nature Conservancy

The Nature Conservancy bills itself as the world's leading conservation organization, with more than 1 million members and activities in thirty countries. It claims to have protected over 117 million acres of land and 5,000 miles of rivers worldwide. The Conservancy adopts a science-based approach to address threats to conservation, whether those threats originate from natural or man-induced causes.

What distinguishes the Nature Conservancy from other conservation organizations is its apolitical stance. It "pursues non-confrontational, pragmatic solutions to conservation challenges." As such, while the Conservancy has been highly involved in issues impacting the Arctic coastal plain of Alaska and Canada, including ANWR and the 1002 Area, it has purposely remained neutral with respect to drilling in ANWR. No doubt its membership has challenged this position, as the Conservancy Web site (www.nature.org) specifically addresses the matter:

> The debate over oil drilling in the Arctic Refuge is highly polarized and divisive. Both sides have very significant values at stake and both sides have brought science to bear in support of their arguments. One of the Conservancy's core approaches is a cooperative, solutions-based approach to conservation. We have carefully evaluated the situation and determined that the most effective and powerful contribution our particular organization can make to conservation of Arctic fish and wildlife is to focus on bringing diverse Arctic stakeholders together rather than further delineating sides.

The Conservancy, a science-based organization, has produced an Alaska-Yukon-Arctic Ecoregional Assessment. This comprehensive study is a biodiversity analysis based on the natural boundaries of the entire Arctic region spanning Alaska and Canada, including the Arctic coastal plain. It transcends any man-made boundaries and therefore better captures the patterns of migratory wildlife. This assessment has apparently proved a useful tool in engaging parties on both sides of the drilling debate, and the intent is to identify areas of significant biological diversity with the aim of balancing conservation with the sustainable development of natural resources. Given the intensity of the debate, this is no easy task. However, the Conservancy has distinguished itself as a conservation organization with a practical approach to problem solving.

Natural Resources Defense Council

The Natural Resources Defense Council (NRDC) is a U.S.-based activist organization. Founded in 1970 by attorneys and law students, it claims 1.2 million members. The headquarters is in New York City, with regional offices in Washington, DC, San Francisco, Los Angeles, Chicago, and Beijing. Heralded by *The New York Times* as one of the nation's most powerful environmental groups, the NRDC takes a legal approach toward addressing environmental issues. Curbing global warming, saving wildlife and wild places, and moving America beyond oil are several of its primary objectives. The NRDC stresses energy efficiency as a substitute for drilling for additional reserves, advocating better fuel efficiency in vehicles as well as better tires that would improve gas mileage.

The NRDC Web site (www.nrdc.org) frames the debate as purely political, with Republicans in favor of leasing in the 1002 Area and Democrats opposed to leasing. While this is largely true, it somewhat oversimplifies the issue. The NRDC is adamantly opposed to drilling in ANWR. Its Web site makes its position clear with headings such as the following:"

"Arctic National Wildlife Refuge: Why Trash an American Treasure for a Tiny Percentage of Our Oil Needs?"

"Arctic Refuge Oil is a Distraction, Not a Solution."

"Handing On to Future Generations a Wild, Pristine Arctic? Priceless."

"Oil Development Damages Air, Water, and Wildlife."

Upon reading further, it becomes clearer as to the underlying concerns and premises by which the NRDC operates:

> The drive to drill the Arctic refuge is about oil company profits and lifting barriers to future exploration in protected lands, pure and simple. It has nothing to do with energy independence. Opening the Arctic Refuge to energy development is about transferring our public

105

estate into corporate hands, so it can be liquidated for a quick buck.

Despite repeated failure and stiff opposition, drilling proponents press on. Why? They believe that opening the Arctic Refuge will turn the corner in the broader national debate over whether or not energy, timber, mining, and other industries should be allowed into pristine wild areas across the country. Next up: greater Yellowstone? Our Western canyonlands? Our coastal waters?

The concern voiced by NRDC is that ANWR could become the defining issue regarding access for, not just energy exploration, but for other extractive industries as it pertains to access to public lands and waters. In other words, ANWR may be the watershed event that triggers opening of other federal lands and offshore waters. With respect to energy exploration, the next target after ANWR could be offshore California, the Florida Gulf Coast, and the Eastern continental shelf.

ANWR is viewed by NRDC, as well as by other conservation organizations, as the definitive "line in the snow."

The Sierra Club

While many environmental organizations started up in the heady activist days of the 1970s, the Sierra Club has roots as far back as 1892. With 1.3 million members, it claims to be the oldest, largest, and most influential grassroots environmental organization in the United States. It was founded by noted environmentalist John Muir.

The Sierra Club is heavily engaged in the dispute over ANWR, listing the region among its "Places in Danger." As a grassroots entity, it urges its members to sign petitions, write letters to decision makers, tell friends and relatives, and submit letters to the local newspapers.

The Web site (www.sierraclub.org) contains numerous sections dedicated to the Arctic in general and ANWR in particular:

"Take Action! Oil Companies Stay Out of the Polar Bear Habitat."

"Big Oil in America's Arctic."

"The Gwich'in: A Way of Life."

"The DespOILed Arctic."

"The Great Polar Bear: Helpless in the Face of Global Warming."

U.S. PIRG

The U.S. Public Interest Research Group (PIRG) "takes on powerful interests on behalf of the American public." The organization operates on a state-by-state basis, with the U.S. PIRG Federation of States based in Boston. Environmental causes are but one of the many positions it undertakes on behalf of the public. Product safety, identity theft, political corruption, prescription drugs, and voting rights are among the many issues it tackles. Its mission is to "deliver persistent, results-oriented public interest activism that protects our health, encourages a fair, sustainable economy, and fosters responsive, democratic government." PIRG's modus operandi is through research, media exposure, grassroots organizing, advocacy, and litigation.

Because U.S. PIRG is multifaceted and more than an environmental/conservation organization, it has tended to align itself with other public interest groups in order to make a bigger statement. With respect to ANWR, in a news release dated April 18, 2002, it joined with Green Century Capital Management and the World Wildlife Fund (WWF) to file a resolution at the BP annual shareholders' meeting to recognize the risks associated with drilling in ANWR. The Gwich'in and Porcupine caribou figure heavily in the resolution. While the resolution was only supported by 11 percent of the shareholders, this was heralded as a victory in the press release.

PIRG also chastised the Bush administration for including $7 billion in the 2008 proposed budget from oil lease bonus payments in ANWR, calling the inclusion highly speculative and irresponsible:

"Drilling for oil in the Arctic National Wildlife Refuge will neither make us energy independent nor generate anywhere close to $7 billion, but it would destroy one of America's last wild places."

World Wildlife Fund

The World Wildlife Fund (WWF) is an international organization founded in 1961, with its headquarters in Switzerland. It claims to be the largest multinational conservation entity in the world, with operations in 100 countries and 5 million members. Membership in the United States is 1.2 million. Its mission is the following:

To preserve the diversity and abundance of life on Earth and the health of ecological systems by:

1 Protecting natural areas and wild populations of plants and animals, including endangered species

2 Promoting sustainable approaches to the use of renewable natural resources

3 Promoting more efficient use of resources and energy and the maximum reduction of pollution

Regarding ANWR and the Arctic coastal plain, the WWF is highly focused on the plight of the polar bear. It supported the U.S. Fish and Wildlife's recent listing of the polar bear as a threatened species under the Endangered Species Act. The WWF Web site, www.worldwildlife. org, contains a summary of its position regarding oil and gas activities in the Arctic as well as a fact sheet on polar bears, including their numbers (20,000 to 25,000) and their habitats (Greenland, Norway, Canada, Alaska, and Russia).

While some of the other conservation organizations resort to hyperbole in discussing drilling in ANWR, the WWF simply states its position in plain terms:

> As we have for more than two decades, WWF will continue to work to preserve the Arctic National Wildlife Refuge in Alaska. WWF, along with our conservation partners, will also advocate for protecting key polar bear habitats from offshore oil and gas development in other parts of the Arctic.

WWF encourages its members to demand that countries with arctic ecosystems manage human activities so as to conserve the biodiversity of the region.

While the issue surrounding the plight of the polar bears and receding sea ice would mostly impact offshore drilling activities, den sites within the Refuge would also fall under protective oversight.

Chapter XII: Pro-Development Constituents

Energy Companies

There are a handful of energy companies that are currently active on Alaska's North Slope and that have, in the past, expressed an interest in ANWR. These are BP, ConocoPhillips, Chevron, Anadarko, and ExxonMobil. While there may be others who would bid on leases in the 1002 Area of ANWR should the opportunity arise, the above companies are the most likely candidates and have the most arctic exploration experience. What makes this group more interesting, however, is their relatively recent low level of interest in ANWR. One has to search far and wide on their respective Web sites to even find a reference to ANWR. And once found, it is often a dated reference, five or more years old. Or it is couched in general terms by calling for opening restricted government lands to exploration.

Opponents of drilling have been quick to recognize this apparent lack of interest and cite this as evidence that there really aren't vast oil reserves to be found in the 1002 Area. To reinforce this claim, they note that Chevron drilled the only exploration well in ANWR in the 1980s, and while the results are still kept confidential, Chevron has not pursued opening ANWR, at least not publicly. This author believes, however, that the energy companies still maintain a strong interest in the 1002 Area, but have elected to adopt a low profile in order to deflect intense public criticism directed at them at annual shareholders' meetings and in the media. Instead, the companies have employed intermediaries to make their position known and to lobby on their behalf. Among the most vocal intermediaries are the American Petroleum Institute (API) and Arctic Power. To bolster this argument, a closer examination of the respective energy companies and their alliances is warranted.

BP

BP is a major oil producer on Alaska's North Slope. The company accounts for more than half of Alaska's oil production. It operates thirteen North Slope fields, including the largest oil field in North America, Prudhoe Bay, with a 26.4 percent interest. In addition, it holds a majority interest, 46.9 percent, in the Trans Alaska Pipeline System (TAPS). BP also has a 30 percent interest in the 35 trillion cubic feet (TCF) of natural gas on the North Slope and is actively engaged in pursuing the development of a natural gas pipeline through Canada to the lower forty-eight states.

Regarding oil in Alaska, BP states that its primary focus is on developing "known" oil resources in and around existing fields. This would theoretically discount wildcat exploration acreage in ANWR. Since BP operates thirteen North Slope fields, this pretty much covers the entire area currently available on the North Slope. BP touts employment of recent technologies, such as miscible gas injection, gas cap water injection, and horizontal drilling, as enabling it to boost recovery rates for oil reservoirs from the usual 35 percent to as high as 60 percent. This is a significant achievement that has extended the life of the North Slope fields and TAPS throughput.

Under FAQs on the BP Web site (www.bp.com), the question of ANWR is directly addressed:

> Is BP for or against the opening of the Alaskan National Wildlife Refuge (ANWR)?
>
> Coastal plain exploration and development is not part of our Alaska business plan. The area is not available for exploration or development and is not the subject of active evaluation.
>
> Plans for growing our Alaska business do not anticipate coastal plain access. We are focused, instead, on the Alaskan opportunities available to the company today. If the Congress and the president agree that energy development in ANWR is in the best interest

of the United States, we will evaluate the opportunity made available by the government, assess it against the other exploration opportunities in our global portfolio, and then decide—on the basis of many factors—whether the coastal plain is a place BP should explore.

As operator for thirteen North Slope oil fields, with a majority interest in TAPS and 30 percent interest in 35 TCF of natural gas, it is difficult to envision a scenario where BP would not aggressively pursue exploration leases in ANWR should the opportunity arise. From an energy analyst's perspective, ANWR would be a solid strategic fit for BP.

ConocoPhillips

ConocoPhillips is the largest oil and gas producer in Alaska and also the largest holder of exploration leases in the state. It maintains a 36.1 percent interest in the Greater Prudhoe Bay Fields, which includes satellite fields, and is operator of Kuparuk Field, which is the second-largest field on the North Slope. It also operates the Kenai liquefied natural gas (LNG) facility and associated gas fields in North Cook Inlet of southern Alaska. Like BP, the company has an interest in TAPS, which transports North Slope crude to the tanker terminal at Valdez in southern Alaska.

Regarding ANWR, little can be found on the company Web site (www.conocophillips.com) that specifically addresses the issue. However, in a January 2007 news item entitled "Edwardsville Community Report," executive vice president for Refining, Marketing and Transportation, Jim Gallogly, addressed the company's position:

> Gallogly commented that The company does not actively seek to drill in ANWR. As a sign of this commitment, in January 2005, ConocoPhillips ended its ties with Arctic Power, a group that is working to have the U.S. government open the ANWR on the eastern side of Alaska's North Slope to oil drilling. Gallogly said that ConocoPhillips sees more potential for energy security in researching environmentally friendly and economical ways to produce our current resources.

A few comments at this juncture. Note the operative words "does not actively seek" in the above statement. Given its position as Alaska's largest oil and gas producer, one must suspect that this position would change if leasing were permitted in the 1002 Area. Like BP, this is a sound strategic fit. Hence, the company has adopted a more passive, wait-and-see approach.

However, ConocoPhillips has also undertaken a dual strategy that distinguishes it from BP as it relates to ANWR. It has significantly increased its stake in the oil sands of Canada's Alberta Province. These oil reserves are massive, but are technically difficult and costly to extract. Referring back to the chapter on Canada, recall that the Canadian government, as a way to induce the U.S. government to keep ANWR closed, recommended that U.S. companies invest in the Alberta oil sands. It appears that ConocoPhillips has done just that. This does not preclude the company from pursuing ANWR if the opportunity arises, but rather provides it with an alternate target in the event ANWR remains closed. Keep in mind that all of the energy companies to be discussed are active members of the American Petroleum Institute, which endorses leasing in ANWR.

Chevron

Chevron operates ten platforms and five natural gas fields in the Cook Inlet of southern Alaska. Mostly through its acquisition of Unocal, the company also holds non-operating interests in several fields on the North Slope and in TAPS. Chevron is the only company to have drilled a well in the 1002 Area of ANWR. As previously mentioned, the KIC#1 well, which was drilled in 1984–1985, remains a "tight hole" (confidential) to this day. As with ConocoPhillips, Chevron has also taken a position in the Athabasca Oil Sands of Alberta Province in Canada.

There is little direct mention of ANWR on Chevron's Web site (www.chevron.com). The most recent is a press release that dates back to the stockholders' meeting of May 15, 2002. At this meeting, a shareholder proposal to report on potential environmental damage to ANWR was defeated by 92 percent of the votes cast.

Prior to that, one can find a June 4, 1998, press release that announces the signing of a long-term exploration lease agreement between Chevron and BP with the Arctic Slope Regional Corporation (ASRC), covering 92,000 acres in the Kaktovik region of the 1002 Area. The exact terms of the agreement were not disclosed, and it is not clear if the lease is still active today. At the time the lease agreement was announced, ASRC President Jacob Adams endorsed the project by stating the following:

> We have worked together for 15 years to evaluate ASRC's mineral interest in the Kaktovik area. Although we cannot specifically comment on details of the U.S. Geological Survey's recent report, we are pleased that they have confirmed that the Arctic National Wildlife Refuge (ANWR) is indeed an area with important energy resource potential, and have endorsed the widely held view that it is one of the few remaining areas in the domestic United States for significant hydrocarbon reserves. We continue to stress the need for the federal government to allow full access to our property.

A decade later, ANWR no longer is mentioned on the Chevron Web site. Instead, the company published its "Energy Policy," which makes oblique reference to ANWR and other inaccessible acreage:

> Governments can help stimulate the development and deployment of new energy technologies, next generation ethanol fuels, and advanced battery systems. However, the most critical role of governments will be to set a policy framework to promote energy and environmental security and to balance these effectively.
>
> We need an energy strategy based on sound management principles that include efficiency, protecting core environments, and investing in the future.
>
> That strategy should reflect new areas of development that are becoming available as a result of our own increased investments and advanced technology. But the delivery of new energy supplies to market is hindered by restricted access and lengthy

regulatory processes in both the United Sates and abroad. Governments should move proactively to address these issues.

This theme of restricted access imposed by the federal government is echoed throughout the energy industry. It recently surfaced at a U.S. Senate Judiciary Committee hearing on June 2, 2008. Energy industry senior executives were called in to address committee concerns over the high price of oil and gasoline. Chevron, as well as North Slope companies BP, ExxonMobil, and ConocoPhillips, were among the lineup. While the intent was no doubt to give the companies a sound drubbing for the high prices, the executives responded by stating that government policies of the past thirty years that have restricted access to prospective energy resources have negatively impacted the domestic supply side of the oil equation. They further stated that this supply decline could be reversed with a change in policy toward lifting federal restrictions on exploration for oil and gas in such areas as Alaska, the continental shelf on the West and East Coast, and the eastern Gulf of Mexico.

Hence, we are starting to see a theme whereby the energy companies broaden their attack on the federal government with respect to restricted access, but do not specifically mention ANWR by name. This tactic is no doubt intended to soften the opposition to exploring in environmentally sensitive regions while engaging both the federal government and the American public on the issue of general access to public lands in order to alleviate high energy prices.

Anadarko

Anadarko is not a major operator on the North Slope, but the company does hold 22 percent interest in Alpine Field and its satellite fields, Fiord and Nanuk. While Anadarko's Web site (www.anadarko.com) lists Alaska under its operational highlights, it is discussed in broad terms of exploring for high-upside prospects along with developing low-risk satellite opportunities. It does mention that it is actively exploring new frontier basins in Alaska, but declines to state which ones those are.

The only specific reference to ANWR occurs in a press release dated May 17, 2001, whereby then-Chairman Robert Allison, Jr., enthusiastically voiced support for the Bush administration's proposed national energy policy:

> We need to open the coastal plain of the Arctic National Wildlife Refuge, the '1002 planning area,' which represents just 8 percent of the total area of ANWR. The new Alpine Field that we developed with Phillips on the North Slope of Alaska—just 60 miles west of ANWR—demonstrates that oil can be developed safely and responsibly in sensitive Arctic environments with very little impact on the environment and no damage. At the Alpine Field, new technology has allowed us to develop the 40,000-acre field from two gravel pads totaling 100 acres.

The theme of doing things better, safer, and with less impact on the environment due to technological advances will be discussed in a later chapter. For now, Anadarko joins its brethren in adopting a low public profile with regard to ANWR.

ExxonMobil

ExxonMobil, the world's largest publicly traded company, has commanded a long-term presence on the North Slope since its partnership with ARCO drilled the Prudhoe Bay discovery well, the State #1, in 1968. It currently holds a 36.4 percent interest in the Greater Prudhoe Bay Fields and smaller interests in a number of North Slope fields, such as Kuparuk, Tarn, West Sak, and Tabasco. In addition, it maintains a 20.3 percent interest in TAPS.

The company's image was significantly tarnished in Alaska and nationally when the tanker *Exxon Valdez* ran aground in Alaska's Prince William Sound in 1989, spilling 11 million gallons of oil. Exxon spent approximately $2.5 billion in damages and clean-up, but the damage to its public image has endured.

Given the impact to its reputation, one would expect ExxonMobil to adopt an extremely low profile with respect to ANWR. Indeed, its Web site (www.exxonmobil.com) provides a virtual cornucopia of policy directives aimed at addressing a multitude of environmentally sensitive issues. However, it is difficult for an 800-pound gorilla to blend in among its fellow corporations with more diminutive balance sheets. Under the general heading of "Crude Oil Supply," the column plainly stated that the key to the future is access:

> Access to areas that have not yet been heavily explored is vital to finding new reserves and to meeting the world's growing energy needs. Competitive access by the world oil industry to previously closed acreage in the former Soviet Union, China, Venezuela, and Brazil has brought major benefits to oil consumers worldwide. Large areas of Europe and the United States, however, remain unavailable to exploration. Today, areas offshore California and Florida, the Alaska National Wildlife Refuge (ANWR), and about 40 percent of all non-park Western lands are off limits.

ExxonMobil is somewhat bolder in directly naming ANWR in its overall theme regarding access to restricted areas with exploration potential. However, the approach is the same as the others: clamoring for a change in government policy.

The American Petroleum Institute

The American Petroleum Institute (API) bills itself as the leading trade association of the U.S. oil and gas industry. It has over 400 members, representing all sectors of the petroleum business. All of the major energy companies operating in Alaska belong to API. Its mission is "to influence public policy in support of a strong, viable U.S. oil and natural gas industry essential to meet the energy needs of consumers in an efficient, environmentally responsible manner."

Hence, it should come as little surprise that API is based in Washington, DC. The primary focus is on influencing federal regulatory and legislative policies, but its reach also extends down to the state level. Because API speaks on behalf of the entire U.S. petroleum industry, it carries far more weight than individual energy companies when it comes to impacting laws and regulations. And in the case with ANWR, API provides a convenient cover for those companies that seek to minimize their individual public exposure while at the same time collectively indicate a strong desire to open the 1002 Area of ANWR.

On its Web site (www.api.org), API makes its case for opening ANWR under the heading "Strategic Energy Resource: ANWR, Alaska." It cites U.S. Geological Survey estimates of oil reserves in ANWR ranging somewhere between 5.7 and 16.0 billion barrels (representing the 5th and 95th percentile distribution, with a mean of 10.4 billion barrels). This is stated to be more than twice the proven reserves in Texas. With production ramping up to 1 million barrels per day (a figure not supported by all analysts), this would be roughly equivalent to the oil imported from less-than-friendly Venezuela, and twice that of oil imported from Russia (based on 2008 monthly imports).

API also states that the federal legislative limit for oil and gas activities in the 1002 Area is restricted to 2,000 acres. This would have been the case if the relevant legislation had been passed by Congress and signed into law. It was not.

The institute does make a good case for the technological advancements and environmental considerations that have taken place since Prudhoe Bay was developed in the 1970s. They range from the reduced size of the development footprint to seasonal limitations on exploration activities, including the implementation of ice roads and airstrips. These improvements are significant and are covered in greater detail in a later chapter.

API echoes the drumbeat of the energy companies by calling for access to federally restricted lands. In the article "History of Northern Alaska Petroleum Development," it stated the following:

> The most significant barrier to realization of the growing resource potential of Northern Alaska has been a policy of consistently over-restrictive limitations on access to Federal land.... Development of those state and native properties has extended to the very boundaries of Federal areas to the East, the West, and the North of current development. Moreover, available geologic information in each of those Federal areas has increasingly suggested that the major resource potential realized on state and native lands likely extends well

into the federal areas, and may actually far exceed the potential of state lands.

As it did a quarter century ago, Northern Alaska today offers the U.S. an opportunity to stabilize, or even increase domestic oil supply. Given the prospects for future world supply, the value of the opportunity today is as great if not greater than it was then.

While not specifically mentioned by name, the federal area to the east would clearly be ANWR, to the west would be the National Petroleum Reserve—Alaska (NPRA), and to the north would be federal offshore.

As the debate over ANWR ebbs and flows, one can expect to see API squarely in the midst of this controversy, with the energy companies closing ranks directly behind, albeit quietly. For now, the individual companies appear most content to let API take the lead, and most of the heat.

Arctic Power

Arctic Power is an Anchorage-based organization, founded in 1992, whose primary purpose is to expedite congressional approvals for exploration and production in the 1002 Area of ANWR. It boasts a membership of 10,000, including the Alaska Oil and Gas Association, state truckers, and forest and miners associations. It also includes Alaska native corporations as well as state and local officials. Arctic Power maintains an extensive Web site (www.anwr.org) and a representative office in Washington.

Although Arctic Power defines itself as a "grassroots, non-profit citizen's organization," the Annenberg Public Policy Center describes it as a coalition of industry groups. In either case, Arctic Power is the only major entity whose sole mission is to open ANWR for leasing. Its Web site does not list individual corporations as members. However, it is noteworthy that both BP and ConocoPhillips dropped their membership in the organization. BP pulled out in November 2002 after a campaign led by Green Century, World Wildlife Fund, and PIRG Arctic Wilderness Campaign threatened shareholder resolutions demanding the company report the risks associated with operating in ANWR. ConocoPhillips withdrew its membership from Arctic Power in January of 2005, ostensibly for the same reasons and under the same threat of shareholder resolutions.

Environmental organizations such as U.S. PIRG lauded the victory and indicated that such actions by the two energy companies suggested that they were not really interested in drilling in ANWR (www. truthout.org). This line of reasoning is inconsistent with behind-the-scenes activities by the energy companies. Simply put, Arctic Power may be a little too "high profile" for the energy companies. With its only focus being leasing in ANWR, it is difficult for the energy companies to be members and, at the same time, deflect the intense pressure inflicted by environmental organizations and shareholder actions. The current strategy by the energy companies is to let associations like the American Petroleum Institute, which has a much broader agenda, carry the standard in the battle for ANWR.

This does not signify that Arctic Power would be rendered impotent if the major North Slope operators shrink from its ranks. The organization still serves as the focal point for Alaska's rank and file to weigh in on the great debate and to make their presence felt in the halls of Congress.

Think Tanks:
The Heritage Foundation and the
National Defense Council Foundation

Washington has an abundance of non-profit 501(C)(3) think tanks whose general mission is to provide in-depth analysis of existing government policies and to hopefully shape the direction of future policies. Although there are many that address energy issues, two are mentioned here as they relate to ANWR: the Heritage Foundation and the National Defense Council Foundation.

The Heritage Foundation is generally regarded as a conservative think tank. Its mission is "to formulate and promote conservative public policies based on the principles of free enterprise, limited government, individual freedom, traditional American values, and a strong national defense." As such, it is somewhat representative of the broader conservative views regarding ANWR. In a December 2, 2005, brief on ANWR, it made its position quite unequivocal:

> Action item: Opening ANWR would be the federal government's first significant pro-energy measure in years and a sign that Washington is finally ready to start addressing the nation's future energy needs. Lawmakers should recognize the benefits of domestic oil production and ANWR's potential to reduce U.S. dependence on foreign oil.

The above statement came shortly after the U.S. House of Representatives struck a provision calling for leasing in the 1002 Area in ANWR from the budget bill.

In contrast to the Heritage Foundation, with its broader policy objectives, the National Defense Council Foundation (NDCF) purports a more focused mission, that of researching energy security, drug wars, and low-intensity conflicts. It has weighed in on the ANWR controversy, basing its involvement on the need to reduce America's dependence on foreign oil, especially oil from potentially hostile regimes or from regions subject to supply disruptions, as in the Middle East.

The National Defense Council Foundation also reported that the United States would gain 2,210,418 jobs, both directly and indirectly, as a result of oil and natural gas development in Alaska. These employment numbers were derived from the foundation's own research (The Economic Impact of ANWR Resources, 2003), so the data cannot be independently verified. Nonetheless, the multiplier effect on job creation as it relates to indirect employment is a recognized phenomenon. The NDCF also lists potential ANWR oil production as achieving rates of 1.6 million barrels per day, a number that is roughly twice as high as is estimated by the U.S. Energy Information Administration.

While perhaps not as prominent as the Heritage Foundation, the National Defense Council Foundation has presented testimony before Congress and has been lauded for its research and advice with respect to matters involving U.S. security.

Chapter XIII: The American Public: Perceptions and Polls

IT IS DIFFICULT TO find any significant national public awareness regarding ANWR prior to 2001. Certainly, the energy companies and leasing advocates were active as far back as the late 1980s, as were the aforementioned opponents. However, the issue did not enter the national psyche until after the terrorist attacks on September 11, 2001. Energy prices shot up dramatically immediately following the attack, and the matter of energy security assumed greater importance throughout the nation, second only to engaging Al Qaeda. Energy also became an issue when Hurricane Katrina struck in the Gulf of Mexico in late August 2005, briefly shutting down production platforms and Gulf Coast refineries. This oil supply disruption was mitigated, however, by temporarily tapping into the Strategic Petroleum Reserve until routine supplies could be re-established.

None of the major events mentioned above, however, galvanized public opinion quite like the dramatic run-up in oil prices in 2007–2008, which exceeded $140 per barrel and sent the prices at the pump over $4.00 per gallon of gasoline and $5.00 for a gallon of diesel. The economic impact on the average American, both in terms of high gas prices and home heating oil, was devastating. Finger-pointing in Congress was elevated to an art form. The energy companies were paraded before congressional panels and grilled as to whether they were price gouging, and the concept of a windfall profits tax was once again proposed. Energy speculators were accused of recklessly running up the price of oil futures while both parties in Congress blamed each other for failing to promote a viable national energy policy.

So did any of the above events serve to heighten the awareness of

Americans about ANWR, and did any of these momentous episodes alter public opinion about leasing in ANWR? The best way, perhaps the only way, to address these questions is by analyzing survey results, commencing with the aftermath of September 11, 2001.

A caveat regarding polls is warranted before we launch into the details. In an endeavor to obtain a desired result, the way questions in some surveys are posed can be leading, or more appropriately, misleading. One has to examine who authorized the particular survey and the manner in which it was conducted in order to assess the accuracy of the survey results and to determine if it truly is representative of the population as a whole. Often, the way questions are phrased can be leading.

Case in point: the Wirthlin Worldwide surveys conducted in September and October 2001, immediately following the attack of September 11. It is important to note that these surveys were commissioned by Arctic Power. The September survey sampled 1,000 American adults over eighteen. One of the questions in the survey was as follows:

"Environmentalists say we should preserve America's last pristine wilderness in Alaska, even if it limits our national security. Do you agree or disagree with this statement?"

Sixty-four percent of respondents either somewhat or strongly disagreed, while 34 percent either somewhat or strongly agreed.

However, the question that immediately preceded the above was:

"Increasing our dependence on foreign oil will make the Saddam Husseins of the world more powerful and America more vulnerable. Do you agree or disagree with this statement?"

Seventy percent either somewhat or strongly agreed.

The above questions established a strong linkage between national security and ANWR. Remember that this survey was conducted in the aftermath of 9/11, where national security took center stage. It is a safe assumption that any program that strengthened national security at that time would most likely be enthusiastically supported by the American public. This is not to say that drilling in ANWR does not have a national security component. It does. How much weight should be given to that component is a matter for debate.

Regrettably, the geographic distribution for the Worthlin Worldwide

September 2001 survey is not available. One could easily envision dramatically different results if the poll was conducted in California versus in Alaska.

A second survey was conducted by Worthlin in October 2001 among 600 voters in the two states of South Dakota and New Mexico. The South Dakota sampling included 85 percent who considered themselves to be strong Democrats, and 91 percent were union households. In New Mexico, 88 percent considered themselves to be strong Democrats, and 88 percent were union households.

Of the South Dakota voters, 67 percent of Republicans versus 43 percent of Democrats felt that the positives of ANWR production outweighed the negatives. In New Mexico, 73 percent of Republicans versus 39 percent of Democrats also said that positives outweighed the negatives. The Republican-versus-Democrat divide comes as no surprise, nor does the fact that most union households are Democrats. And since most of those surveyed considered themselves to be strong Democrats, it can be assumed that a valid statistical sampling of South Dakota and New Mexico would suggest most citizens of those states would oppose drilling in ANWR.

In 2002, after energy prices somewhat stabilized (a relative term), the great debate over leasing the 1002 Area in ANWR played out mostly on Capitol Hill, with peripheral interest being maintained mainly by the stakeholders, including environmental organizations. Public interest took a back seat for the time being, until 2005.

In 2005, the Republican-dominated Congress made numerous attempts to attach ANWR leasing provisions to energy and budget bills, all without success. The pollsters came to life throughout this process.

In a January 2005 poll conducted by Republican firm Bellwether Research and by Democratic firm Lake, Snell Perry and Associates for the Alaska Coalition (which opposes leasing in ANWR), the question was posed:

"Should oil drilling be allowed in America's Arctic National Wildlife Refuge?"

Fifty-three percent of the 1,003 telephone survey respondents were opposed to oil drilling in ANWR, while only 38 percent were in favor and 10 percent were undecided.

Given that this survey was viewed as being bipartisan, it was considered fairly definitive and served to show that public opinion had firmed regarding ANWR, and that most American did not want ANWR open for leasing. In fact, there was strong sentiment against drilling, with 44 percent of respondents strongly opposed to leasing and 73 percent agreeing with the statement that the issue of drilling in the Arctic Refuge is "too important to the American public and future generations to be snuck through in the budget process."

At nearly the very same time period as the above poll, several other surveys came out with dramatically different results. A January 2005 poll by Harris Interactive found that 53 percent of respondents would support "energy reform that would allow companies to drill for oil in such areas as the Arctic National Wildlife Refuge (ANWR) to decrease our reliance on foreign oil." The difference of opinion once again stood along party lines, with 80 percent of Republicans in favor of drilling, while 59 percent of Democrats were opposed.

Another poll conducted by Republican pollster Frank Lutz on behalf of Arctic Power, also in January 2005 (January 2005 was a banner month for pollsters), produced results similar to the Harris survey. A slim majority of 53 percent of respondents favored leasing in ANWR. Upon listening to points favorable to drilling, this number increased to 67 percent. The fact that an argument was put forward to persuade survey participants to change their minds, in this writer's opinion, taints this particular poll. Untainted, however, the results are consistent with the Harris poll that was conducted at the same time.

Interestingly, a December 2004 Zogby International poll commissioned by the Wilderness Society found that 55 percent of those surveyed opposed drilling in ANWR and that only 38 percent were in favor.

The apparently conflicting results between the various polls led the Environment News Service to headline an article, "ANWR: You Get What You Poll For." If one were to discount those polls commissioned by both opponents as well as advocates of leasing, then perhaps the bipartisan survey that was jointly conducted by Republican and Democratic polling firms is most representative of the public sentiment in January 2005. Hence, a slim majority of Americans (53 percent) were against drilling in ANWR.

This position was reasserted in June 2005 with a national telephone poll of 1,002 Americans jointly conducted by *The Washington Post* and ABC News. Of those surveyed, 49 percent opposed drilling while 48 percent supported drilling in ANWR. Fearing a gradual decline in support of their cause, environmental groups named June 11, 2005, as "Arctic Action Day" with documentaries and media events planned in Washington.

While the June 2005 survey represents a narrower margin of opposition than the bipartisan survey of the previous January, one observation can safely be made: Given the plethora of surveys and media attention in 2005, Americans had become more aware of ANWR than at any other time in its history.

Fast-forward to 2008. Energy prices experienced an unprecedented run-up. Gasoline, diesel, and home heating oil costs had a crippling effect on the nation's economy, and the American consumer was sent reeling from the impact. President Bush and congressional Republicans renewed their call for leasing in ANWR as well as to lift the moratorium against drilling in federal waters. ANWR made almost daily news by drilling proponents and opponents alike. The public is more aware of ANWR than ever. Did public opinion shift in light of these developments?

The Pew Research Center, a non-partisan think tank, conducted a telephone survey of 1,508 adults in February of 2008. At that time, 50 percent of respondents still opposed drilling in ANWR, with only 42 percent in favor. The number of people who did not know, 8 percent, suggests that most Americans are now fully aware of ANWR and the issues. As could be expected, approximately twice as many Republicans were in favor of leasing as compared to Democrats. Interestingly, more men (51 percent) favored drilling, as contrasted with only 35 percent of women respondents. Age apparently also makes a difference, with those fifty and older in favor of drilling, while those under fifty were in opposition.

Just a few months later, in June 2008, a Zogby International telephone survey of 1,113 likely voters nationwide found that 59 percent of respondents favored drilling in ANWR and 74 percent supported more offshore drilling in U.S. coastal waters. Republicans, by an overwhelming 90 percent, favored leasing ANWR, while only

40 percent of Democrats felt the same way. Importantly, 57 percent of independents now supported drilling in ANWR.

From June 18 to 29, 2008, the Pew Research Center conducted another nationwide survey of 2,004 adults. As contrasted with its earlier survey in February, the results were nearly the exact opposite. While the February survey indicated 50 percent of participants opposed drilling in ANWR, now the June survey showed only 43 percent opposed. Likewise, the June survey showed 50 percent were now in favor of drilling as compared to only 42 percent last February.

Perhaps even more significant, in Pew polls dating back to 2001, this is the first time that respondents stated that it is a more important priority to expand exploration drilling and mining and the construction of new power plants than it is to call for increased energy conservation and regulation. A full 60 percent felt that it was a higher priority for the country to develop new energy resources, compared to 34 percent that said that protecting the environment was a higher priority. This latter point regarding priorities cuts across all age groups, indicating a definite shift in priorities by people under age fifty in favor of expanded energy exploration.

Republican sentiment regarding ANWR had also increased, to a full 75 percent favoring exploration (versus 63 percent in February 2008). Democrat resistance softened only by about 5 percent (64 percent still oppose), while independents increased their support from 41 percent in February to 48 percent in June 2008.

Amazing how $4.00-per-gallon gasoline can sharpen one's priorities.

By late 2008, the price per barrel of oil was hovering around $40, with a resultant dramatic drop in gasoline and heating oil prices. Energy was no longer at the forefront of the political debate, taking a backseat to the banking crisis, home foreclosures, and jobs. ANWR once again dropped from the public consciousness.

Chapter XIV: Rhetoric versus Reality

THE RESEARCH INTO THIS book began as a simple desire to learn what ANWR was all about and to develop a more comprehensive understanding of the issues surrounding the great debate as to whether the 1002 Area of ANWR should be opened for exploration and development. What I discovered is that there was an abundance of rhetoric coming from all quarters, and very little factual information. Worse, with what scant information was publicly available or pronounced in the media, the facts were often heavily distorted. Hence this book, a good-faith attempt to separate rhetoric from reality with respect to ANWR so that the readers can decide for themselves as to what course of action should be pursued. This chapter endeavors to address the most striking rhetorical, or misleading, elements regarding ANWR in a terse, straightforward manner, as follows:

Rhetoric: There are 10 billion barrels of oil in ANWR just waiting to be produced.

Reality: We see this number often quoted by leasing advocates. The fact is, we don't really know how much oil is, or isn't, in ANWR. The number 10.36 billion barrels represents the mean estimate of technically recoverable reserves made by the U.S. Geological Survey and is based on very little technical data. It is based on 1,400 miles of two-dimensional (2-D) seismic data acquired in the 1980s and by analogy to existing hydrocarbon production on the North Slope. This is a minuscule amount of seismic data when considering it encompassed the 1002 Area of 1.5 million acres plus state waters.

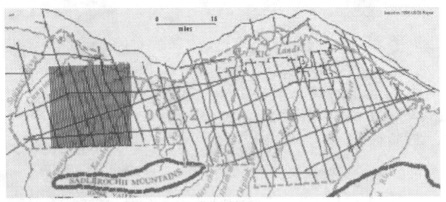

➤Impact lines from 2-D seismic exploration in 1984-85.
▥▥Typical line spacing for 3-D seismic exploration, overlaid on part of the coastal plain for comparison.

Seismic lines in ANWR: map courtesy of USGS

The USGS essentially did their best with what they had to work with, but it by no means confirms the presence of massive amounts of oil. In fact, the 10.36 billion barrel estimate covers the entire assessment area, which includes native lands and state waters within the three-mile limit. The federal 1002 Area has a mean reserve estimate of 7.668 billion barrels, not the 10.4 billion that is often quoted.

Part of study area	Volume of oil, in millions of barrels		
	F_{95}	Mean	F_{05}
Entire assessment area[1]	5,724	10,360	15,955
ANWR 1002 area (Federal), TOTAL	4,254	7,668	11,799
Undeformed part	3,403	6,420	10,224
Deformed part	0	1,248	3,185

[1] Includes 1002 area shown on figure 2, Native lands, and adjacent State water areas within 3-mile boundary (see fig. 2).

ANWR 1002 Area oil reserve estimates: courtesy of USGS

Perhaps more importantly, however, is the possible range of recoverable reserves. The USGS estimate a 95 percent probability of reserves being greater than 5.724 billion barrels and only a 5 percent probability of reserves being greater than 15.995 billion barrels. Put another way, there is a 95 percent probability that recoverable reserves over the entire assessment area will be less than 16 billion barrels.

It is critical to note that the above-referenced reserves will not all be found in one place, and that commercial field sizes will range from several billion barrels to less than 100 million barrels, with the lower limit highly dependent on the price of oil.

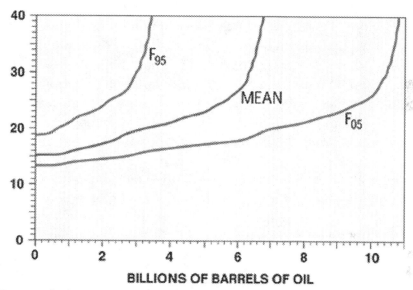

RESOURCE COSTS-ANWR 1002

Impact of oil price on commercially recoverable oil reserves: courtesy of USGS

Therefore, when you hear the number 10 billion barrels being quoted, understand that it could be significantly more or less, and that this number includes native lands within the 1002 Area and state waters out to the three-mile limit.

This is an appropriate juncture to mention that once oil or gas is discovered and developed, it generally leads to more nearby discoveries and additional reserves. Once the expensive infrastructure is in place, it allows for smaller fields to be considered commercially viable. Prudhoe Bay was initially calculated to contain 10 billion barrels of recoverable oil. It is now believed to be 13 billion.

Reserves grow for a variety of reasons. It could be as simple as reservoir engineers making conservative reserve estimates of a field's potential at the outset. This is a common practice and not necessarily a bad thing, because reserve estimates are scrutinized by independent auditors and regulatory agencies. If the energy company is publicly traded, shareholder investments are often predicated on field size estimates. To overestimate reserves could bring charges of fraud and ensuing litigation.

Reserve growth can also come from newer technologies that enhance both primary and secondary recovery techniques, such as horizontal drilling, three-dimensional (3-D) and four-dimensional (4-D) seismic, reservoir stimulation, and gas reinjection for pressure maintenance. Hence, instead of only recovering around 35 percent of in-place oil, recoveries often will approach 65 percent. This is a dramatic increase.

In addition, reserves are often found by drilling deeper, or by stepping out from an existing field to drill on an adjacent structure, or by employing new technology to find an overlooked reservoir in an already-drilled area.

Rhetoric: We can't drill our way out of this energy crisis.

Reality: While on the face of it this statement appears true, no reputable source ever stated that we could drill our way out of the energy crisis. This is a highly disingenuous remark made by opponents of leasing because it presumes that energy policy advocates only want to drill for oil in ANWR and the offshore waters in the lower forty-eight states. Drilling is but one component of a fundamental energy policy that would include solar, wind, clean coal, geothermal, biofuels, and nuclear components.

Closely related to the above comment is the following:

Rhetoric: Opening ANWR won't solve today's energy crisis. It will take eight to ten years to produce any oil we discover there.

Reality: This statement is often quoted by political opponents of leasing during times of high energy prices when immediate relief is mandated. It is precisely the same leasing opponents who have blocked drilling in ANWR over the years. Thus, it becomes a self-fulfilling prophecy. While the statement is true on its face, it lacks historical perspective. In 1995, Congress passed legislation that would have opened the 1002 Area of ANWR for leasing. It was then vetoed by President Clinton. Had the bill been signed into law, it is highly probable that a discovery in ANWR would already be in production.

Rhetoric: Oil companies aren't drilling on existing leases. Why give them more?

Reality: This statement reflects a fundamental lack of understanding as to how an energy company operates, but it was a popular campaign slogan in the 2008 elections. Essentially, it was designed to counter calls for lifting drilling restrictions on federal lands, including ANWR. The Barack Obama campaign Web site even devoted a paragraph to this notion, as follows:

> Oil companies have access to 68 million acres of land, over 40 million offshore, which they are not drilling on. Drilling in open areas could significantly increase domestic oil and gas production. Barack Obama and Joe Biden will require oil companies to diligently develop these leases or turn them over so that another company can develop them.

The above statement would have one believe that energy companies are knowingly not developing oil fields just to drive up the price of oil. The truth is the following:

- Not all leases result in an oil or gas discovery. That is why energy companies drill wildcat wells. Wildcat wells generally have a success rate of 10 to 20 percent. Many leases are non-productive.

- Energy companies prioritize their prospects, and drill or drop the acreage depending on the prospectivity of the lease area.

- Exploration leases already have term limits. Leases are either partially relinquished or entirely turned back after a set period.

- Leases are generally acquired after paying a bonus to the mineral owner, sometimes in the millions. In addition, annual rental payments are made to the mineral owner, whether it be the federal government, the state, or a private owner. This payment occurs even if no oil or gas is produced.

Rhetoric: *The energy companies only need 2,000 aces of the 19.3 million acres in ANWR.*

Reality: While field development footprints have been significantly reduced since Prudhoe Bay, multiple field discoveries within the 1002 Area would most likely require more than 2,000 acres. This number has been included in numerous attempts by Congress to pass leasing legislation, no doubt hoping that the small amount of acreage would placate leasing opponents. It hasn't worked.

One development scenario has the primary production processing facilities all situated on native Alaskan lands, thereby excluding it from the 2,000-acre figure. This is misleading because it represents one of many possible development scenarios. The location of a major discovery will be a determining factor in the placement of the production facilities, pipelines, living quarters, roads, and airstrip.

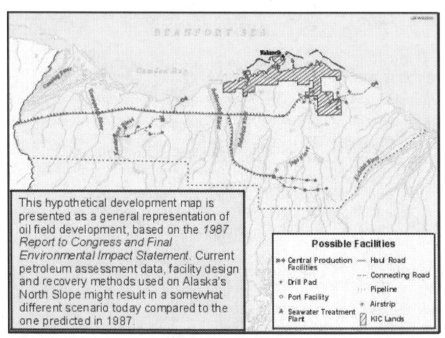

This hypothetical development map is presented as a general representation of oil field development, based on the *1987 Report to Congress and Final Environmental Impact Statement*. Current petroleum assessment data, facility design and recovery methods used on Alaska's North Slope might result in a somewhat different scenario today compared to the one predicted in 1987.

Possible Facilities

●● Central Production Facilities	— Haul Road
● Drill Pad	∼∼ Connecting Road
○ Port Facility	⋯ Pipeline
▲ Seawater Treatment Plant	✴ Airstrip
	▨ KIC Lands

Hypothetical field and facilities development map: courtesy of USFWS

One should view the 2,000-acre limitation for what it is: an attempt to get a foothold in ANWR. Once there, it would be difficult to oppose the development of a major discovery simply because it exceeded the 2,000-acre limit. Amendments would be made, possibly in piecemeal fashion. All sides to this debate should honestly view consideration of the 1002 Area as open for future development in its entirety, save for environmental restrictions.

Rhetoric: ANWR is a frozen wasteland or America's Serengeti.

Reality: It is a little bit of both. Leasing proponents will stress that there is very little life in ANWR's coastal plain, especially during the winter months when temperatures are well below freezing and ice and snow blanket the plain. I can still recall Alaskan Senator Ted Stevens showing a picture of ANWR in winter, which was nothing but white on a piece of poster board. It portrayed an image of a barren, featureless landscape, hostile to all living creatures.

However, the U.S. Fish and Wildlife Service have identified 249 species of vertebrates that inhabit or migrate through the Arctic National Wildlife Refuge. This consists of 36 kinds of fish, 8 marine mammals, 169 birds, and 36 terrestrial mammals. Granted, not all of these species transit the 1002 Area of the coastal plain; some reside farther to the south in the Brooks Range. Still, one could hardly characterize this as a wasteland.

ANWR coastal plain in summer: photo courtesy of USGS

At the same time, environmentalists will often refer to ANWR's coastal plain as America's Serengeti. This is in reference to the Serengeti National Park in Tanzania, which consists mainly of grassy plains and sparsely treed savanna. The Serengeti is known for its migration of more than a million wildebeest and several hundred thousand zebra and is home to numerous species. The Serengeti National Park is also listed as a UNESCO World Heritage Site because of its biodiversity and ecological significance. While certain parallels with ANWR are obvious, such as migratory herds and grassy plains in the summer months, the scale and abundance of wildlife in the Serengeti far surpasses that which exists on ANWR's coastal plain. A more suitable comparison for the Serengeti might be made with the Great Plains of the Midwest.

Rhetoric: Drilling in ANWR will have only a minimal impact on the price of gas at the pump.

Reality: Nobody really knows. Leasing critics have often made the above claim, adding that the reduction would only amount to a few cents per gallon. This is generally followed by the comment that it would then be ludicrous to destroy a pristine ecosystem for the sake of a few pennies. The basis for this statement derives its origin from a 2005 Energy Information Administration report entitled "Impacts of Modeled Provisions of H.R. 6 EH: The Energy Policy Act of 2005." This report attempts to model energy prices, including oil and motor gasoline, into the year 2025. In 2025, the modeling does actually predict a drop of only about one cent per gallon of gasoline if ANWR were to add another 1 million barrels to domestic supply. The problem with the model is that it is based on the assumption that a barrel of oil in 2025 will only cost about $30 (in 2003 dollars) against a baseline 2003 price of $27.73 per barrel. This report was conducted prior to the ramp-up in energy prices in 2007–2008, when oil prices exceeded the EIA estimates by as much as fourfold. Hence, the report would have to be greatly modified to reflect actual prices and can only predict what might happen in the year 2025.

Leasing advocates will claim that production from ANWR could reduce the price of a gallon of gas by as much as 50 cents. A related corollary is that ANWR production will lower the price of crude oil.

It is essential to bear in mind that any production from a discovery in ANWR would not come on line for roughly eight to ten years. Only by knowing what the oil and gasoline supply-and-demand equations reveal, how much oil America consumes, how much of that oil is imported, and how much of that oil is refined into gasoline *a decade from now* can we even begin to address the issue of price reduction at the pumps.

On a related note, limited domestic refining capacity could also impact the price of gasoline. Hence, even if the oil is readily available, should gasoline demand outstrip our ability to refine the oil into gasoline, one can expect higher prices at the pump.

One should also keep in mind that oil is refined not just for gasoline, but for diesel fuel, jet fuel, home heating oil, lubricants, and other refined products. The table below depicts the breakdown of an average barrel of oil, which demonstrates that gasoline represents less than half of a barrel when refined. Note that this is a generalized depiction only for purposes of this discussion.

Product	Gallons Per Barrel
Gasoline	19.4
Distillate Fuel Oil	10.5
Kerosene –Type Jet Fuel	4.1
Coke	2.2
Residual Fuel Oil	1.7
Liquefied Refinery Gases	1.5
Still Gas	1.8
Asphalt and Road Oil	1.4
Raw Material for Petrochemicals	1.1
Lubricants	0.4
Kerosene	0.2
Other	0.4

Source: Energy Information Administration

Perhaps a better way to leave this issue is to honestly state that all sides agree that oil production from ANWR will have some impact on the price of gasoline and other refined products when it eventually enters the marketplace, but the exact impact cannot be accurately quantified at this time.

Rhetoric: Drilling in ANWR is essential to America's energy security by reducing our dependence on foreign oil.

Reality: There is some truth to this. Increased domestic oil and natural gas production from any sector would decrease our reliance on foreign sources, thus providing some added degree of energy security. However, it should not be overstated. According to the Energy Information Administration, we import roughly 60 percent of our oil as of 2008. Of that 60 percent, approximately half comes from countries located in the Western hemisphere, primarily Canada, Mexico, and Venezuela. The remainder of imported oil is spread throughout the globe, including Africa, Russia, and the Middle East.

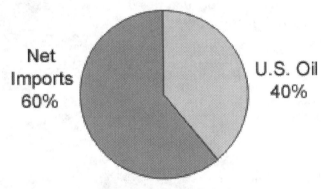

Source: Energy Information Administration

2008 oil imports vs. domestic U.S. production

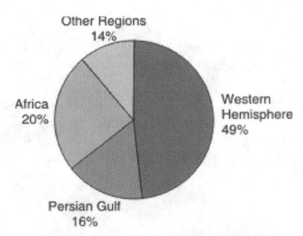

2008 distribution of oil imports to the United States

Crude Oil Imports (Top 15 Countries)
(Thousand Barrels per Day)

Country	May-08	Apr-08	YTD 2008	May-07	YTD 2007
CANADA	1,840	1,952	1,889	1,821	1,841
SAUDI ARABIA	1,579	1,453	1,531	1,574	1,402
MEXICO	1,116	1,259	1,207	1,461	1,469
VENEZUELA	1,030	1,019	998	1,232	1,103
NIGERIA	851	1,115	1,053	882	1,047
IRAQ	583	679	670	341	458
ANGOLA	464	579	468	680	581
ALGERIA	440	393	329	496	495
BRAZIL	318	201	209	152	170
KUWAIT	263	176	227	162	182
COLOMBIA	245	149	184	104	101
ECUADOR	162	160	194	201	200
RUSSIA	119	106	86	232	156
LIBYA	96	85	73	33	51
EQUATORIAL GUINEA	93	40	58	0	52

Source: Energy Information Administration 2008

Several of the oil suppliers to the United States are far from staunch allies. This would include countries such as Venezuela and Russia, while others remain neutral at best.

The major benefit voiced by leasing proponents is that oil from ANWR would help to reduce our dependence on foreign oil and thus prevent the United States from being held hostage by unfriendly oil-producing countries. This is true to a degree. Certainly, producing more oil domestically does reduce our dependence on foreign oil. Could foreign nations hold the United States hostage by withholding oil? This is somewhat unlikely, because oil is a global commodity that is traded on the global marketplace. If we can't buy oil from one country, we can buy it from another. However, should a consortium such as OPEC decide to limit or reduce production for political reasons, we could witness a detrimental impact on energy prices in the United States, and this could alter U.S. foreign policy. Historically, however, OPEC has experienced difficulty in limiting production, with individual OPEC member countries often exceeding their established quotas.

The more likely scenario is that there would be supply disruptions, whether through natural causes such as natural disasters or human induced, such as through conflict. Under these circumstances, increased domestic oil supplies, whether it be derived from ANWR, offshore, or elsewhere in the United States, would indeed have a stabilizing effect.

Rhetoric: Opening ANWR would result in massive revenues and job creation.

Reality: This statement is speculative at best. Revenues could be substantial, firstly from lease bonuses as energy companies vie for exploration licenses within the 1002 Area. Estimates as high as $5 billion for lease bids have been projected. Much of the remainder of the revenue stream would come from royalty payments on any production, and corporate taxes from profits on the sale of the oil. We won't have a realistic assessment of these major components of the revenue stream until discoveries are made and reserves can be quantified. Therefore, estimates that project combined state and federal revenues of $60 billion (National Defense Council Foundation) on the first fifteen years of production are premature. Not to say that it would not occur, but that it would be dependent on a number of factors, the price of oil at time of production and the cost to extract being but two of those factors.

Estimates for job creation have been reported as high as 2.2 million from Alaskan oil and gas resource development (National Defense Council Foundation), of which ANWR would be a major component. Job creation would supposedly occur in every state, with California gaining as many as 334,435 new jobs. It is difficult to envision such a large number of new jobs arising from a discovery in ANWR.

Rather than challenge every estimate, however, it might be more instrumental to view this through the various phases of an exploration and development project. In the initial exploration phase, seismic and drilling crews are employed. Materials utilized during this phase might result in new positions, and it is conceivable that additional seismic crews, drilling crews, and related service company personnel would be formed. However, since most of these service companies already exist, job creation would not be significant. The economic impact would most likely be localized to Alaskan-based companies and the local economy.

Once a discovery is made, however, development activities would engage a much larger job force. More drilling crews, service companies, and equipment would be required. Production facilities, processing plants, pipelines, and roads would need to be constructed. Job creation would reach its zenith during this phase. New positions would be created locally, and materials and equipment would be manufactured by many companies throughout the States. It is not beyond the pale to envision the creation of thousands, and even tens of thousands, of new jobs during this development phase, which would last several years.

Once in production, however, the number of positions would be dramatically reduced. As the construction winds down, small crews of production technicians and maintenance personnel are generally all that is required to keep a production facility running. The numbers are small and would be similar to the exploration phase of the project.

To sum, the largest ramp-up in new jobs would be confined to the development phase of the project where production facilities are constructed, lasting less than five years. Even if the multiplier effect for new jobs is considered, this author still has some difficulty in confirming the 2.2 million figure.

Rhetoric: Drilling on the coastal plain of ANWR would destroy a pristine arctic ecosystem and imperil wildlife that live or migrate there.

Reality: Once again, there is some truth to this exaggeration. It suggests, however, that any development will most certainly destroy the delicate arctic ecosystem. It would be more plausible to state that there is a reasonable concern that human activity in ANWR could have a detrimental impact on the ecosystem and wildlife.

Critics of the above rhetoric will argue that oil development on the remainder of the North Slope has not harmed wildlife there. In fact, the Central Arctic caribou herd has increased in numbers since development began. In addition, the 1002 Area only represents about 8 percent of ANWR, much of which is already protected with a Wilderness Area designation.

Two of the largest mammals that inhabit the coastal plain are the polar bear and Porcupine caribou. Energy companies would be wise not to downplay their potential impact on these mammals, lest their credibility be damaged even further.

The polar bear recently received additional protection under the Threatened and Endangered Species Act as a threatened species. The U.S. Fish and Wildlife Service has identified twenty-two polar bear den sites in the 1002 Area and continues to monitor the bears' activities as they relate to ANWR. There is a legitimate concern that seismic operations, which involve multiple vehicles, noise, and vibrations, could disrupt the bears in their winter dens and result in early displacement of the bears, thus exposing the cubs to the harsh arctic winter. Any exploration and development activities would have to take these den sites into account in order to satisfy environmental regulations under the act.

The Porcupine caribou herd migrates and calves along ANWR's coastal plain. Estimates of the size of the herd range in the neighborhood of 123,000 to 160,000, with most settling around 125,000. The caribou are not threatened or endangered, and hunting is allowed. Most hunting is conducted by the Gwich'in on the Canadian side of the Arctic coastal plain, while the Gwich'in from Alaska's Arctic Village to the south of ANWR also rely on the Porcupine caribou as part of their subsistence. In total, the Gwich'in of Alaska and Canada take about 3,000 caribou a year, with the Alaska contingent taking roughly 300 caribou, or 10 percent of the total.

The U.S. Fish and Wildlife Service claim that a reduction of only 5 percent of the calf survival rate could imperil the viability of the herd. Pipelines, roads, and production facilities could impact access to calving and post-calving and insect relief areas, as well as alter migratory patterns. Hence, even if the Porcupine caribou are not a protected species, safeguarding their viability would need to be addressed.

While the oil companies operating on the North Slope appear to enjoy a somewhat favorable reputation regarding wildlife preservation, stricter standards may need to be applied with respect to protecting wildlife in new exploration areas.

Rhetoric: Companies operating on the North Slope will abandon their fields once reserves are depleted, leaving an environmental disaster in their wake.

Reality: This is simply false. This claim comes from the notion that strict field abandonment and habitat restoration regulations were not legislated at the time Prudhoe Bay was being developed. Therefore, energy companies would not be legally bound to clean up after themselves once fields were depleted.

This author believes that omission to be a good thing for the following reason: When Prudhoe Bay was first discovered in 1968, the environmental movement was just getting started. The knowledge base regarding arctic ecosystems and wildlife habitat was far less than it is today, and it will be somewhat greater in the future when the North Slope fields deplete their reserves. Any regulations derived at the time of Prudhoe Bay would pale in comparison to environmental regulations mandated now and in the future. In other words, the energy companies will now face much stricter field abandonment and habitat restoration laws, with which they must comply.

Will there still be some vestige of human past production activities on the North Slope once the oil and gas is gone? Almost certainly, but it will be far smaller than one could have envisioned back in 1968.

Chapter XV: Possible Solutions

PERHAPS THE MOST OBVIOUS question posed regarding drilling in the 1002 Area of ANWR should be, "Is there room for compromise?"

Apparently not, at least not thus far.

Congress and the executive branch have had an abundance of opportunities over several decades to effect compromise legislation, including the caveat to restrain development to 2,000 acres and to dedicate government revenues to alternative energy research and the betterment of native Alaskans. Despite repeated calls for lifting restrictions on drilling in July 2008 by the Republican minority in Congress, ANWR was once again dropped from the agenda, leaving only the offshore areas up for discussion. It is difficult to envision a compromise scenario that would be considered more appealing to leasing opponents while simultaneously remaining feasible to leasing advocates.

ANWR has, for the most part, been viewed as an all-or-nothing proposition.

Then what other possible solutions to the dilemma might exist?

In order for either side to bring this matter to a close, whether it be opened for leasing or forever declared an off-limits Wilderness Area, both the Congress and the administration would have to be on the same page, which normally implies the same party. In addition, the leading party in Congress would have to have a sufficient majority to break a filibuster by the minority. In the event the administration is of an opposing party, a majority in Congress would be required to override a presidential veto. The 2008 national elections brought a Democrat to the White House and stronger Democratic majority in both houses of Congress. Thus, it is conceivable that the Obama administration could propose a permanent drilling ban for ANWR, with Congress introducing legislation for a permanent Wilderness designation to include the 1002 Area. However, it is far from certain that Senate Democrats could prevent a filibuster on the bill, despite their numbers. And not all Democrats would necessarily favor the bill.

Are there any other options? Yes, but none are easy.

One option would be to propose an acreage exchange with another area that is deemed equally worthy of preservation. For want of a better name, let's call this the **"Energy Offsets Proposition."** Put simply, the concept would be to open the 1002 Area of ANWR in exchange for closing another area of similar value.

There exist federal lands that are currently open to drilling, logging, and mining interests that could be considered for a permanent Wilderness designation. In the case of offshore areas, these could receive a Marine Sanctuary designation. For example, the federal canyon lands in Utah that are currently open for leasing could be considered for such an exchange. Other areas that could be substituted would be federal waters offshore California, or the eastern Gulf of Mexico, or the outer continental shelf on the East Coast.

Critics of this plan may contend that ANWR represents a unique arctic ecosystem and that it simply cannot be exchanged for another property elsewhere. This point is valid to a degree. A Wilderness Area in the Rocky Mountains, for example, does not contain the exact same ecological characteristics as ANWR's coastal plain. However, the other property would still be considered both unique and highly valuable from an environmental perspective. Equal, but different. Unique, but of equal import. The areas need not be of the exact same size. In fact, it is the natural bounds of the specific ecosystem that should dictate the area involved, not a political boundary drawn by a regulatory agency.

A practical issue that arises regarding this proposition, however, is that of determining value. Who decides what is of equal value? The Department of the Interior? The Environmental Protection Agency? Energy companies and Environmental organizations? Congress? One can envision another twenty years spent in debating this question alone. As a practical matter, one could suggest that the Department of the Interior act as lead agency, with relevant input from such agencies as the U.S. Fish and Wildlife Service, the U.S. Geological Survey, environmental organizations, and relevant industries.

How likely is it that the Energy Offsets Proposition would be given serious consideration? It is difficult to say. Some parties may favor this approach, while others may view it as simply shifting the issue from one controversial site to another. Some may judge it more advantageous to hold the line at ANWR now that the government and the nation are aware to some degree of the issues and the stakes. Besides, this proposal has an air of compromise to it. As stated previously, there appears to be little room for compromise. The battle lines have been drawn.

At the same time, permanently removing environmentally desirable areas from commercial consideration would elicit a highly favorable response from conservation organizations. The advantage in an Energy Offsets Proposition is that this proposal can be applied to all other federal lands that are considered prospective for petroleum development, not just ANWR. Taken a step further, this model can also apply to mining and logging on federal acreage. In the author's opinion, the concept of offsetting future development by preserving another sensitive area strikes a real balance and merits contemplation. Implementation of the Energy Offsets Proposition would require the enactment of congressional legislation.

Another option, however, would be to take the decision out of the hands of Congress. After all, they had over two decades to resolve this matter, and the only result has been divisiveness, rancor, massive expenditures, stalemate, and unconscionable rhetoric by all parties. Opponents of leasing may view this stalemate as positive, for so long as there is no action, there is no drilling. However, the possibility of future exploration still exists, and the call for action reaches fever pitch whenever energy prices impact the average consumers, also known as voters. A stalemate is not a permanent solution.

The mechanism for commanding the legislative branch of government to take action on an issue would be by an initiative or legislative proposition. This process is not to be confused with its close relative, the referendum. A referendum is the process where voters cast ballots to accept or reject a law already enacted by the legislature. An initiative is more proactive in its nature. According to the Initiative and Referendum Institute at the University of Southern California, an initiative is defined as a proposal of a new law or constitutional amendment that is placed on the ballot by petition. The petition is a collection of signatures from citizens who can legally vote in the specific jurisdiction where the initiative is proposed.

The first impediment to this option is that there is no provision in the U.S. Constitution for a national initiative. Hence, U.S. citizens, as a nation, cannot petition the federal government to take action on ANWR, whether it be for or against drilling. Instead, the initiative process must be conducted on a state-by-state basis. For the initiative to work, individual states would have to petition to place ANWR on the state ballot.

This raises the second impediment. Not all states allow for an initiative. Currently, only twenty-four states permit initiatives, including Alaska. However, all states allow for a legislative measure or legislative proposition, where the state government places a proposal on the ballot for a decision by the voters. Therefore, at least twenty-four states could take the initiative route, with the remaining twenty-six states going by way of legislative proposition. Alternatively, all fifty states could follow the legislative proposition process.

Finally, we come to the third impediment to this somewhat grandiose option. Even if individual states arrive at a collective decision regarding the future of ANWR, that decision does not automatically transform itself into a federal mandate. ANWR is federally protected land, and Congress, by law, is the only governing body empowered to enact legislation impacting it.

So how would the initiative or proposition process be of any help in resolving this issue?

The answer lies in how the initiatives or propositions are worded. The wording should not direct the state government to take action regarding ANWR. Rather, the wording should direct the U.S. Senators and Representatives of that state to either sponsor or support federal legislation regarding ANWR, whether it be for or against drilling, based on the voters in their state. Essentially, every eligible voter would have a say in the outcome. Some states might indicate that the proposition could be advisory only as it applies to their U.S. delegation to Congress. But a politician would be loathe to ignore the advice of a majority of his or her constituency.

The initiative or legislative proposition approach is by no means a simple mechanism to employ, and it would take considerable time and effort to mount a campaign simultaneously in all fifty states. Yet despite the impediments discussed above, this plan has merit in that it levels the playing field by marginalizing the special interest groups on all sides, and it leaves the decision of ANWR up to the citizens whose land it ultimately belongs.

Chapter XVI: Conclusion

IT IS EASY TO lose oneself in the complex myriad of issues surrounding the Arctic National Wildlife Refuge. There is the widely discussed potential impact on the wildlife, whether endangered or not, encompassing all those that inhabit or migrate through the Refuge. There are climatic concerns, issues about use of fresh water for ice roads and drill pads and the strain on rivers and streams and the fish therein. There are concerns about destruction of the tundra and impacts on native Alaskan villages that reside in or around ANWR. And despite vastly improved technological advances since Prudhoe Bay, there are anxieties about oil spills and field abandonment obligations. Is there a little or a lot of oil? Will it make a difference at the pump?

One aspect of closing ANWR and other restricted areas to exploration is that it hastens, albeit painfully, the movement toward implementation of alternative energy sources. It is poignant to observe that once gas prices exceeded $4.00 per gallon, many consumers traded in their SUVs and pickup trucks for hybrids and more fuel-efficient vehicles. Additionally, some users of home heating oil either supplemented with or switched to residential solar heat or wood stoves. Another ancillary benefit is that more federal and state funding is now available for alternative energy programs.

At the same time, there are concerns about our growing dependence on foreign oil and being held hostage by oil-exporting countries hostile to the United States. There are concerns about the impact of high oil prices on the U.S. economy, especially as they roll down to the consumer, impacting both income and jobs. The state of Alaska and the majority of its citizens, including native Alaskans, also harbor real fears of being deprived of much-needed revenues and jobs if leasing does not occur.

One could go on and on, countering one argument with another. However, in the interest of all parties, it might be more productive, assuming one actually desires an outcome as opposed to dragging this debate on for another twenty years, to frame the essence of the debate in a single thought:

Environmental preservation of an arctic ecosystem as measured against energy security.

Should the 1002 Area of ANWR be forever preserved as a Wilderness Area or should it be made available for petroleum exploration in order to reduce our dependence on foreign oil? Most Americans can get their arms around that concept. If they want to know more, there are numerous sources that can be consulted, including this book and the references contained therein.

One final aspect of ANWR has yet to be mentioned. It never comes up in any discussions, whether for or against leasing. One has not heard our representatives in Congress echo this thought aloud, no doubt out of fear that it might actually galvanize public opinion in one direction or the other. Yet it is no doubt lurking in the deeply recessed thought process of the stakeholders to this great debate as it plays out on the national theater.

Put simply: As ANWR goes, so goes the nation.

In other words, should the 1002 Area of ANWR be leased, it would open the door for leasing in other potential exploration areas that are currently restricted. This would include offshore California and the outer continental shelf of the East Coast. It would include the eastern Gulf of Mexico. It would also include restricted lands in the Rocky Mountain region and elsewhere.

Why is this the case? Because opponents of leasing, such as conservation organizations, have made ANWR their foremost rallying cry for environmental protection. And politicians in states like California and Florida have taken up that banner. They are fully aware that if ANWR falls to development, then California or Florida would likely become the next targets as pro-development constituents shift their focus to the lower forty-eight states. And after exhausting every argument against leasing and losing in ANWR, there would not be any additional points to be made, nothing new that would halt the onward advance of pro-leasing advocates. This is a proposition unthinkable to many politicians and stakeholders, yet it is not a difficult scenario to envision.

That is why ANWR has become a **"line in the snow."**

References

"Agreement Between the Government of Canada and the Government of the United States of America on the Conservation of the Porcupine Caribou Herd." July 17, 1987. articcircle.uconn.edu/ANWR

"Alaskans Support Opening ANWR's Coastal Plain." 2003. Poll results conducted by Dittman Research Corporation, February. Downloaded April 25, 2008. www.anwr.org/features/support.htm

American Museum of Natural History. Earth Bulletin, "No Place Like ANWR." earthbulletin.amnh.org/D/1/2/

American Museum of Natural History. Earth Bulletin, "Why ANWR?" earthbulletin.amnh.org/D/1/1/

ANWR Assessment Team. 1999. "The Oil and Gas Resource Potential of the Arctic National Wildlife Refuge, 1002 Area, Alaska." U.S. Geological Survey Open File Report 98-34.

"Arctic National Wildlife Refuge: The Gwich'in of Alaska and Canada." Downloaded April 27, 2008. arcticcircle.uconn.edu/ANWR

Attanasi, E. D. 2005. "Undiscovered Oil Resources in the Fedcral Portion of the 1002 Area of the Arctic National Wildlife Refuge: An Economic Update." U.S. Geological Survey Open-File Report 2005-1217.

Attanasi, E. D. 2005. "Economics of 1998 U.S. Geological Survey's 1002 Area Regional Assessment: An Economic Update." U.S. Geological Survey Open-File Report 2005-1359.

Bates, R. L., and Jackson, J. A. (Eds.). 1987. *Glossary of Geology*. Alexandria, Virginia: American Geological Institute.

Bird, K. J., and L. B. Magoon (Eds.). 1987. "Petroleum Geology of the Northern Part of the Arctic National Wildlife Refuge, Northeastern Alaska." *U.S. Geological Survey Bulletin, volume 1778*.

"Canada Offers United States Alternatives to ANWR." 2001. *Petroleum News Bulletin*, February 22. www.petroleumnews.com

Canadian Embassy. Washington, 2001. "A Unique Ecosystem at Risk." News release, October 11. www.canadianembassy.org/environmental

Canadian Embassy. 2001. "Letter to Members of the U.S. House of Representatives from Ambassador Michael Kergin." News release, July 17. www.canadianembassy.org/environmental

Cannon, J., and Lee, Y. 2006. "Alaska Economic Trends: A 10-Year Industry Forecast." State of Alaska, Department of Labor and Workforce Development. November.

Clough, N. K., P. C. Patton, and A. C. Christiansen (Eds.). 1987. "Arctic National Wildlife Refuge, Alaska, Coastal Plain Resource Assessment. Report and Recommendation to the Congress of the United States and Final Legislative Environmental Impact Statement." Washington, DC: U.S. Fish and Wildlife Service, U.S. Geological Survey, and Bureau of Land Management. Volume 1.

Cole, T., and Cravez, P. 2004. "Blinded by Riches: The Prudhoe Bay Effect." University of Alaska, Anchorage: Institute of Social and Economic Research. February.

Congressional Record Service. 2005. "ANWR and FY2006 Budget Reconciliation Legislation." CRS Report for Congress RS22304, October 19.

Congressional Record Service. 2005. "Legislative Maps of ANWR." CRS Report RS22326, November 18.

Congressional Record Service. 2006. "Arctic National Wildlife Refuge (ANWR): Controversies for the 109th Congress." Issue Brief for Congress IB10136, January 26.

Congressional Record Service. 2007. "Arctic National Wildlife Refuge (ANWR): New Directions in the 110th Congress." CRS Report RL 33872, February 8.

Congressional Record Service. 2008. "Arctic National Wildlife Refuge (ANWR): Legislative Actions, 95th Congress to 110th Congress." CRS Report RL32838, September 2.

Gislason, E. Date uncertain. "A Brief History of Alaska Statehood (1867–1959)." xroads.virginia.edu.

Griffith, B., Douglas, D. C., Walsh, N. E., Young, D. D., McCabe, T. R., Russell, D. E., White, R. G., Cameron, R. D., and Whitten, K. R. 2002. "The Porcupine Caribou Herd." In D. C. Douglas, P. E. Reynolds, and E. B. Rhodes (Eds.), "Arctic Refuge Coastal Plain Terrestrial Wildlife Research Summaries," pp. 8–37. U.S. Geological Survey, Biological Resources Division, Biological Science Report USGS/BRD/BSR-2002-0001.

Gwich'in Steering Committee, The Episcopal Church, and Wilson, R. J. 2005. "A Moral Choice for the United States."

Montgomery, S. L. 2005. "Petroleum Geology and Resource Assessment: 1002 Area, Arctic National Wildlife Refuge." *American Association of Petroleum Geologists Bulletin*, Volume *89*, Number 3. March.

National Academy of Sciences. 2003. "Cumulative Environmental Effects of Oil and Gas Activities on Alaska's North Slope." March.

National Defense Council Foundation. 2003. "The Economic Impact of Developing ANWR Resources." Alexandria, Virginia: NDCF.

Obama-Biden Official Campaign Web Site. 2008. "New Energy for America Plan." November. www.barackobama.com

Public Land Order 2214. 1960. "Establishing the Arctic National Wildlife Refuge." F.R. Doc. 60-11510, December 6, filed December 8, 1960.

Ruskin, L. 2001. "Analysts Doubts Forecast of Oil Jobs." *Anchorage Daily News*, September 3, p. A1.

State of Alaska. 2007. "Governor Palin Urges U.S. Senators to Defeat Bill Designating ANWR as Wilderness." Governor Press Archive No. 07-223. Letter from Governor Palin to Senator Joseph Lieberman, November 9. gov.state.ak.us/archive

State of Alaska, Department of Labor and Workforce Development. 2008. Monthly unemployment rate, March. almis.labor.state.ak.us/

State of Alaska, Permanent Fund Dividend Division. Downloaded April 16, 2008. www.pfd.state.ak.us/

Government Agencies
U.S. Department of Energy. 2002. "The Effects of the Alaska Oil and Natural Gas Provisions of H.R.4 and S.1776 on U.S. Energy Markets." Energy Information Administration, February.

U.S. Department of Energy. 2004. "Analysis of Oil and Gas Production in the Arctic National Wildlife Refuge." Energy Information Administration, March.

U.S. Department of Energy. 2004. "Arctic National Wildlife Refuge." Natural Gas Facts, Office of Fossil Energy, National Energy Technology Laboratory, June. Policy006.pmd.

U.S. Department of Energy. 2005. "Bodman Statement On Senate Approval of ANWR Provisions." Office of Public Affairs, News Release, March 16.

U.S. Department of Energy. 2005. "Impacts of Modeled Provisions of H.R. 6EH: The Energy Policy Act of 2005." Energy Information Administration, July.

U.S. Department of Energy. 2006. "Statement from Secretary Bodman on the House Passage of the American-Made Energy and Good Jobs Act." Office of Public Affairs, News Release, May 31.

U.S. Department of Energy. 2006. "Alaska Natural Gas Needs and Market Assessment." National Energy Technology Laboratory, June.

U.S. Department of Energy. 2007. "Potential Impacts of Climate Change on the Energy Sector." National Energy Technology Laboratory report DOE/NETL-403/101807, October 18.

U.S. Department of Energy. 2008. "Statement of Katherine Fredriksen, Office of Policy and International Affairs, U.S. Department of Energy, Before the Energy and Resources Committee, United States Senate." Office of Policy and International Affairs, February 26.

U.S. Department of the Interior. 1983. "Interior Secretary Watt Announces Huge Addition to Arctic National Wildlife Refuge." News release, October 20.

U.S. Department of the Interior. 1987. "Arctic National Wildlife Refuge, Alaska, Coastal Plain Resource Assessment: Recommendation of the Secretary of the Interior to the Congress of the United States." April.

U.S. Department of the Interior. 1987. "Secretary Hodel Says Oil and Gas Leasing on Coastal Plain Would Be Consistent with Protection of Wildlife at Arctic National Wildlife Refuge." News release, April 20.

U.S. Department of the Interior. 1988. "Department of Interior Releases Final Impact Statement on Proposed ANWR Land Exchanges." News release, December 15.

U.S. Department of the Interior. 2006. "Interior Secretary Kempthorne Announces Proposal to List Polar Bears as Threatened Under Endangered Species Act." News release, December 27.

U.S. Department of the Interior. 2008. "Secretary Kempthorne Announces Decision to Protect Polar Bears Under Endangered Species Act." News release, May 14.

U.S. Environmental Protection Agency. 2008. "About EPA." January 25.
www.epa.gove/epahome/about epa.htm

U.S. Environmental Protection Agency. 2008. "2007-2011 Region 10 Strategy: Clean, Affordable Energy and Climate Change." March 18. yosemite.epa.gov/r10

U.S. Environmental Protection Agency. 2008. "Regional Priorities—Oil and Gas." March 14. yosemite.epa.gov/r10

U.S. Fish and Wildlife Service. Date unknown. "Arctic National Wildlife Refuge, Refuge History." arctic.fws.gov

U.S. Fish and Wildlife Service. 1988. "Arctic National Wildlife Refuge Final Comprehensive Conservation Plan, Environmental Impact Statement, Wilderness Review, and Wild River Plans." September.

U.S. Fish and Wildlife Service. 2001. Potential impacts of proposed

oil and gas development on the Arctic Refuge's coastal plain: Historical overview and issues of concern. Web page of the Arctic National Wildlife Refuge, Fairbanks, Alaska. 17 January 2001.
http://arctic.fws.gov/issues1.html

U.S. Geological Survey. 2001. "Arctic National Wildlife Refuge, 1002 Area, Petroleum Assessment, 1998, Including Economic Analysis." Fact Sheet FS-028-01, April..

U.S. Geological Survey. 2002. "Evaluation of Additional Potential Development Scenarios for the 1002 Area of the Arctic National Wildlife Refuge." Director's memo, April 4.

U.S. Geological Survey. 2002. "Supplemental Information Regarding Our Report *Arctic Wildlife Coastal Plain Terrestrial Wildlife Summaries.*" Director's memo, April 5.

Volz, M. 2006. "ANWR remains closed; Gwich'in celebrate." *Indian Country Today*, January 3, Associated Press. www.indiancountry.com

Executive Branch
White House. 2007. "Energy for America's Future." Downloaded February 19, 2007. www.whitehouse.gov/infocus/energy

White House. 2007. "Fact Sheet: Energy Independence and Security Act of 2007." News release, downloaded December 19, 2007. www.whitehouse.gov/news/releases/2007

White House. 2007. "President Bush Signs H.R. 6, the Energy Independence and Security Act of 2007." News release, downloaded December 19, 2007. www.whitehouse.gov/news/releases/2007

White House. 2008. "Energy for America's Future." Downloaded February 29, 2008. www.whitehouse.gov/infocus/energy

White House. 2008. "President Bush Delivers State of the Union Address." News release, downloaded January 28, 2008. www.whitehouse.gov/news/releases/2008

White House. 2009. "Energy and the Environment." Downloaded February 12, 2009. www.whitehouse.gov

Congress

U.S. Senator Barbara Boxer. 2008. "The Environment: Senator Boxer's Environmental Record and Positions." Downloaded March 25, 2008. boxer.senate.gov/issues/environment

U.S. Senator Joseph Lieberman. 2007. "Lieberman Leads Opposition to Drilling in ANWR." News release, downloaded November 7, 2007. lieberman.senate.gov/newsroom

U.S. Senator Lisa Murkowski. 2008. "Alaska: Issues Statement." Downloaded March 25, 2008. murkowski.senate.gov/public

U.S. Senator Ted Stevens. 2007. "Alaska's Congressional Delegation Vows to Defeat Anti-Development Legislation." News release, downloaded November 7, 2007. stevens.senate.gov/public

U.S. Senator Ted Stevens. 2008. "Senators Stevens and Murkowski Introduce Legislation to Open ANWR." News release, downloaded March 13, 2008. stevens.senate.gov/public

U.S. Congressman Edward Markey. 2005. "Remarks of Rep. Markey, Arctic Refuge Action Day." Downloaded September 20, 2005. markey.house.gov/index

U.S. Congressman Don Young. 2008. "Hot Issue: Congressman Don Young: A Leading Voice on Natural Resources." Downloaded March 25, 2008. donyoung.house.gov/HotIssue

Stakeholders

Alaska Coalition
www.alaskacoalition.org

Alaska Communities, Arctic Village Alaska
www.ilovealaska.com

Alaska Federation of Natives
www.nativefederation.org

American Petroleum Institute
www.api.org

Anadarko Corporation
www.anadarko.com

Annenberg Public Policy Center
www.annenbergpublicpolicycenter.org

Arctic Power
www.anwr.org

BP Corporation
www.bp.com

Center for Biological Diversity
www.biologicaldiversity.org

Chevron Corporation
www.chevron.com

ConocoPhillips Corporation
www.conocophillips.com

Environmental Defense Fund
www.edf.org

ExxonMobil Corporation
www.exxonmobil.com

Green Century Funds
www.greencentury.com

Greenpeace
www.greenpeace.org

Heritage Foundation
www.heritage.org

Initiative and Referendum Institute at the University of
Southern California
www.iandrinstitute.org

Natural Resources Defense Council
www.nrdc.org

Nature Conservancy
www.nature.org

Sierra Club
www.sierraclub.org

U.S. PIRG
www.uspirg.org

World Wildlife Fund
www.worldwildlife.org

Polls

Bellweather Research and Lake, Snell Perry and Associates for the Alaska Coalition Poll. Released February 2005. www.usgovinfo.about.com

Frank Luntz and Harris Interactive Polls. Released January 2005. www.ens-newswire.com

Pew Research Center Poll. Released March 6, 2008. www.people-press.org

Pew Research Center Poll. Released July 1, 2008. www.people-press.org

Washington Post-ABC News Poll. Released June 8, 2005. www.anwrnews.blogspot.com

Wirthlin Worldwide Poll. Released September 2001. www.anwr.org

Zogby International Poll. Released June 20, 2008. www.zogby.com

Index

A

ABC News, 125
Adams, Jacob, 113
air quality, 7, 29, 36
Alaska
    economic benefits for, 79–80,
        138–139
    federal public lands in, 99
    job growth in, 82, 120, 138–
        139
    oil discovery in, 14
    population of, 80
    sentiments of, 80–82
    statehood for, 11–12
    as territory, 9–10
Alaska Coalition, 98–99, 123
Alaska National Interest Lands
        Conservation Act
        (ANILCA), 14–15, 25
Alaskan Federation of Natives
        (AFN), 92
Alaskan Native Claims
        Settlement Act (ANCSA),
        13–14, 31, 83
Alaska Oil and Gas Association,
        118

Alaska Permanent Fund
        Corporation (APFC), 80
Alaska Wilderness League, 99,
        100
Alberta oil sands, 95, 112
Allison, Robert, Jr., 114–115
Alpine Oil Field, 7, 83, 114, 115
American Energy Independence
        and Security Act, 76
American-Made Energy and
        Good Jobs Act, 73–74
American Petroleum Institute
        (API), 109, 112, 116–
        118, 119
American public opinion, 121–
        126
America's Serengeti, 103, 133–
        134
Anadarko Corporation, 109,
        114–115
Annenberg Public Policy Center,
        118
Archangelsk Geologia, 1, 5
ARCO International, 1, 3, 4–5,
        115
Arctic Coastal Plain Domestic
        Energy Security Act, 79

Arctic National Wildlife Refuge
    (ANWR)
    creation of, 13–15
    human activity within, 29,
        139
    hydrocarbon potential of, 17–
        23, 117, 127–130
    lands adjacent to, 29–30
    mining within, 29
    offshore development of, 30
    permanent Wilderness
        designation for, 26, 68,
        74–75, 98, 143–144
    private holdings within,
        30–31
    upper Jago River area of, 25,
        28, 52
arctic peregrine falcon, 41
Arctic Power, 91, 110, 111, 118–
    119, 122, 124
arctic sea ice, decreasing, 42–44
Arctic Slope Regional
    Corporation (ASRC), 14,
    31, 83–84, 92, 113
Arctic Village, 53, 88–91, 92,
    140
Attanasi, E.D., 21

B

Ballinger-Pinchot affair, 10
Barter Island, 35, 84
Bartlett, Bob, 12
Beaufort Lagoon-Icy Reef-
    Kongakut River, 35, 36
Begich, Mark, 77

Bellwether Research, 123
Biden, Joseph, 59, 131
birds, 30, 39, 40–41
Bodman, Samuel, 63–64
bowhead whales, 41, 101
Boxer, Barbara, 74
BP Corporation, 109, 110–111,
    113, 114, 118
British North America Act, 9
Bush, George W., 57–59, 63, 67,
    95, 107, 125

C

Canada
    Alberta oil sands of, 95, 112
    against ANWR development,
        93–95
    British North America Act
        and, 9
    Mackenzie Delta, 20, 21, 37
    Northern Yukon National
        Park, 26
    Porcupine caribou herd in, 49,
        51, 52, 53
caribou. *See* individual species
cat trains, 6, 7
Center for Biological Diversity,
    100–101
Central Arctic caribou herd, 46,
    52, 53, 139–140
Chandler Lake Land Exchange
    Agreement, 31
Chevron Corporation, 102, 109,
    112–114
Chretien, Jean, 95

climate, 35–36
Clinton, Bill, 57, 64, 77, 130
coastal lagoon environment, 35
Coastal Plain Local Government
    Impact Aid Assistance
    Fund, 79
Cole, Terence, 79
Colville River Delta, 83
commercially recoverable
    reserves, 19, 129–130
Comprehensive Conservation
    Plan, 17, 25–31, 33, 36,
    46
congressional activity, 67–77
Congressional Research Service
    (CRS), 68
ConocoPhillips Corporation, 83,
    102, 109, 111–112, 114,
    118–119
conservation organizations,
    97–108
Cravez, Pamela, 79

D

Distant Early Warning (DEW)
    Line, 11
Doyon, Ltd., 31
drill pads, 6, 21

E

ecosystems, 33–35
Eisenhower, Dwight, 11, 12

Endangered Species Act (ESA),
    43–44, 101, 108, 140
energy companies, 109–116, 131
Energy Independence and
    Security Act, 58
Energy Information
    Administration (EIA), 62,
    64–66, 120, 134, 136
Energy Offsets Proposition,
    144–145
energy prices, 59, 114, 121, 123,
    125, 134–135, 145
energy security, 26, 57–59, 63,
    101, 121, 136–138, 150
Environmental Defense Fund
    (EDF), 101–102
environmental footprints, 6–7,
    21
environmental impact statements
    (EISs), 6, 25–31
environmental organizations,
    97–108
Environmental Policy Act, 25
Environmental Protection
    Agency (EPA), 67
executive government, 57–59
ExxonMobil Corporation, 102,
    109, 114, 115–116
Exxon Valdez, xiii, 115

F

federal agencies, 59–67
field abandonment, 141, 149
fish, 26, 39, 40
    See also wildlife

footprints, environmental, 6–7, 21
foreign oil suppliers, 136–138, 149
Fredriksen, Katherine, 64

G

Gallogly, Jim, 111
gasoline prices, 59, 114, 121, 125, 126, 134–135, 149
geology, 36–38
Gorbachev, Mikhail, 2
gravel mining, 29, 31
Green Century Capital Management (GCCM), 102–103, 107, 118
Greenpeace, 103
Groat, Charles, 61–62
Gwich'in people, 88–91, 92, 93–94, 98, 100, 107, 140

H

Harris Interactive, 124
Heritage Foundation, 119–120
Hodel, Donald P., 26–27, 51, 60
House of Representatives votes, 68–70
H.R.39 (Udall-Eisenhower Arctic Wilderness Act), 74, 98
Hurricane Katrina, 121
hydrocarbon plays, 20

I

initiative process, 145–147
International Porcupine Caribou Board, 94
In This Place, 86–88
Inupiat Alaskans, 83–88, 90–91, 94–95, 100

J

job creation, 82, 120, 138–139
Johnson, Lyndon, 12

K

Kaktovik Inupiat Corporation (KIC), 14, 31, 83
Kaktovik Village
    Inupiat Alaskans of, 84–88
    private land of, 31, 92
    regional corporations for, 83
    subsistence living by, 40, 41, 44, 53, 86
    U.S. Department of the Interior and, 27
Kempthorne, Dirk, 43–44, 46
Kergin, Michael, 93
KIC #1 well, 84, 112
Kongakut River, 35
Kuparuk Field, 4, 46, 111

L

Lake, Snell Perry and Associates, 123
legislative history, 67–74
legislative proposition process, 145–147
Lieberman, Joseph, 74, 81
Luntz, Frank, 124

M

Mackenzie Delta, 20, 21, 37
mammals, 28, 30, 39, 41–47, 140
    See also individual species
Marine Mammal Protection Act, 43–44
Markey, Edward, 74–75, 98
McCain, John, 82
Minerals Management Service (MMS), 30
mining, 29, 31
Montgomery, Scott L., 20, 37
Muir, John, 106
Murkowski, Lisa, 75–77
musk-oxen, 26, 29, 33, 44, 45–46

N

National Defense Council Foundation (NDCF), 82, 119, 120, 138

National Petroleum Reserve-Alaska (NPR-A), 10, 66, 118
native Alaskans, 27, 83–92, 100, 143, 149
natural gas development, 19, 22, 66, 110, 111, 112
Natural Resources Defense Council (NRDC), 105–106
Nature Conservancy, 103–105
1964 Wilderness Act, 26
North Cook Inlet, 111, 112
Northern Yukon National Park, 26
North Slope
    environmental improvements on, 6–7
    geology of, 36–38
    working conditions of, 2, 4–5
North Slope Borough, 79, 86, 88

O

Obama, Barack, 59, 131, 143–144
Office of Fossil Energy, 62–63
oil
    exploration activities for, 6, 21
    foreign suppliers of, 136–138, 149
    prices for, 21, 121, 125, 126, 134–135, 149
    refined products from, 135

P

Palin, Sarah, 81–82
Permanent Fund, 79–80, 82
Pew Research Center, 125, 126
PIRG Arctic Wilderness
        Campaign, 118
polar bears, 41–44, 98, 101, 108,
        140
polls, 122–126
Pombo, Richard, 65
Porcupine caribou herd
    under Canadian protection,
        93–94
    Gwich'in people and, 88–89,
        90, 91
    potential impact on, 27, 28–
        29, 46, 49–54, 107,
        140
    range of, 33, 49
    size of, 26, 49
Prince William Sound, 115
Prudhoe Bay
    Central Arctic caribou herd
        in, 46
    description of, 1–7
    energy companies interest in,
        110, 115
    geology of, 37
    impact on wildlife in, 76
    oil discovery in, 14
    oil production in, 17, 129
Public Interest Research Groups
        (PIRGs), 102
public opinion, 121–126
Putin, Vladimir, 5

R

Ramstad, Jim, 98
Rayburn, Sam, 12
recoverable reserves, 18–19, 20,
        127–130
referendums, 145
regional corporations, 13–14, 31
    See also Arctic Slope Regional
        Corporation (ASRC);
        Kaktovik Inupiat
        Corporation (KIC)
road construction, 29
Russian delegation, 1–5

S

Seaton, Fred, 13
Senate votes, 71–73
September 11, 2001 terrorist
        attacks, 121, 122
Serengeti National Park, 133–
        134
Seward, William, 9
shareholder advocacy, 102–103
Sierra Club, 106–107
Stevens, Ted, 75–77, 133
Strategic Petroleum Reserve, 58,
        64, 121
surveys, 122–126

T

Teamsters Union, 82

technological advances, 6–7, 117, 149

Teshekpuk Lake herd, 53

think tanks, 119–120, 125

threatened species, 43, 140

Timan Pechora Basin, 1, 5

Trans Alaskan Pipeline System (TAPS)
  capacity of, 22–23
  caribou and, 46
  energy companies interest in, 110, 111, 112, 115
  extending life of, 65
  at Prudhoe Bay, 4, 17

U

Udall-Eisenhower Arctic Wilderness Act (H.R.39), 74, 98

Unocal, 112

U.S. Bureau of Land Management, 17

U.S. Department of Energy (DOE), 62–66

U.S. Department of the Interior, 27, 42–44

U.S. Energy Information Administration (EIA), 62, 64–66, 120

U.S. Environmental Protection Agency (EPA), 67

U.S. Fish and Wildlife Service (USFWS)
  against ANWR development, 59–61
  ANWR under jurisdiction of, 13, 15
  Comprehensive Conservation Plan of, 17, 25–31, 33, 36, 46
  Environmental Impact Statement of, 25–31, 52
  Inupiat Alaskans and, 87
  polar bears and, 41, 108, 140
  species identification by, 39, 133

U.S. Geological Survey (USGS)
  neutral position of, 61–62
  on the Porcupine caribou herd, 53–54
  resource assessment of, 17–23, 117, 127–128

U.S. Public Interest Research Group (PIRG), 107, 119

U.S.-Russia Polar Bear Conservation and Management Act, 43

V

vegetation, 39

W

Washington Post, 125

waterfowl, 30

water quality, 7, 29, 36

wildcat wells, 19, 21, 22, 110, 131

Wilderness Society, 124
wildlife
    abundance of, 26, 39, 133
    birds, 30, 39, 40–41
    habitats for, 28–29
    mammals, 28, 30, 39, 41–47,
        140
    See also fish
wildlife organizations, 97–108
Wirthlin Worldwide, 122–123
World Wildlife Fund (WWF),
        107–108, 118

Y

Young, Don, 75, 77

Z

Zogby International, 124, 125–
        126